MW01673588

Note:

This is all make-believe. Any resemblance to actual persons is purely accidental, except for the actual persons mentioned. Those are intentional as hell.

To be clear.

Cede Catalogue

(giving up already?)

by Cecil Bothwell

Brave Ulysses Books
2021

Cede Catalog

ISBN: 978-1-0881-1300-4

Copyright © 2021 by Cecil Bothwell
All rights reserved/ Cover design by the author

Brave Ulysses Books
POB 1877
Asheville, North Carolina 28802
braveulysses.com

also by the author

•Gorillas in the Myth: A Duck Soup Reader
2000/second edition 2008

•The Icarus Glitch: Another Duck Soup Reader
2001

•Finding Your Way in Asheville
2005/2007/2009/2013/2015

•The Prince of War: Billy Graham's Crusade for a Wholly Christian Empire
2007/ second edition 2009

•Garden My Heart: Organic Strategies for Backyard Sustainability
2008

•Pure Bunkum: Reporting on the life and crimes of Buncombe County Sheriff Bobby Lee Medford
2008

•Can we have archaic and idiot? 2, A collection of fictitious tropes
2009

•Whale Falls: An exploration of belief and its consequences
2010

•She Walks On Water: a novel
2013

Usin' the Juice: Songs, Sermons & Soliloquies
2017

•Fifty Wheys to Love Your Liver: Another collection of fictitious tropes
2018

•Seize You on the Dark Side of the Moo: Still more fictitious tropes
2019

Waist Not, Want Knot
2020

Self Evident: We Hold These Tooths
2021

Cede Catalogue

"Don't it always seem to go?"

à Michele, à Michele

donner-donner

"Therefore I do not wish to consider
any proposition to cede our holdings
to the Great Father."

Sitting Bull

"When defeat is inevitable
it is wisest to yield."

Marcus Fabius Quintilianus

"I think it's weird that the news cedes
so much ground to Wikipedia.
That isn't true in other informational sectors."

Ezra Klein[1]

---

1 Per Wikipedia, Ezra Klein (born May 9, 1984) is an American progressive journalist, blogger, and political commentator who co-founded *Vox*, where he is an editor-at-large. (This should be updated. He now works for The Grey Lady®.)

Foreword

Here we go again! A deep dive from a perilous height..

No doubt you've found yourself lying awake at night wondering what on earth I've been up to and I do appreciate your concern. Someone's got to watch out for me or I could do some serious damage.

Right out of the gate I can assure you that the title of this collection will be explained on page 13 and that the theme will be maintained throughout.

Ralph Waldo Emerson famously said, "A foolish consistency is the hobgoblin of little minds, adored by little statesmen and philosophers and divines. With consistency a great soul has simply nothing to do. He may as well concern himself with his shadow on the wall." So the second thing of which I am at some pains to explain is that my consistency is not foolish. It's more like the nougat in a Three Musketeers® bar.

Mr. Emerson concluded the statement from which the above quote was extracted by saying, "To be great is to be misunderstood." I'm confident that 191 pages from now you will be completely confused and therefore find yourself drawn to label me accordingly. I can live with that.

As for shadows on the wall: "Plato's cave." OK?

Some will come away from this olio thinking that I'm not a serious person, but they will be quite mistaken. I take humor every bit as seriously as the next fellow, and I think we both know how seriously he takes *everything*.

But how do I find time to write many dozens of short stories? [And note that this collection takes my published output somewhere north of 160.] You're in luck! I've come to the point in my motley and peripatetic journey that I feel compelled to share some authorial secrets, knowing that many of my readers will find themselves drawn to traipse in my footsteps. You'll find tips scattered throughout these pages and here's the first.

Tip #1. I purchased a robotic vacuum! Time saved? You betcha!

[A more practical bit of advice for those who believe they have a book inside, itching to escape, is lurking on page 101.]

It's been my great good fortune to make my living as a writer from time to time. I was asked for a resume recently which gave me occasion to consider my trajectory over seven decades and recall that I've always had a pen, a typewriter or a computer near at hand, and through my adult years generally had a project underway.

In grade school I contributed poems and stories for our quarterly *Lines from Lincoln* and recall getting a B on one poem I wrote about a deer, in 6th grade. Undeterred I turned it in again in my new school the following year and nabbed an A, my first inkling that critics are best ignored.

I wrote speeches and tried my hand at a novel in high school, edited my college literary journal, wrote and performed songs as a solo act and band member, published a song book, wrote my first novel, started slamming poetry and freelancing news reporting, wrote and performed a one-person history of the world from 320 BC to 3:20 p.m. yesterday, wrote humor columns for a local monthly, did a weekly radio commentary for a few years, had a nationally syndicated column for a decade, founded/edited an environmental journal for Warren Wilson College, became managing editor of Asheville's *Mountain Xpress,* did a weekly radio news, commentary and music show for five years, was briefly editor for *Asheville City Paper,* and am now again hosting a weekly radio show.

Along the way I've published collections of essays and speeches, biographies, a collection of columns dealing with organic gardening, a novel, a memoir that dipped into philosophy and, for ten years, a city guide: *Finding Your Way in Asheville.*[2]

That last one actually generated some meaningful cash before smart phones supplanted the market for handy guides.

In recent years I've been more and more taken with short fiction. As Edgar Allan Poe observed more than a century ago—modern life is so frantic that short stories are the obvious fiction of the future. [Reminding us of Mark Twain's "If I had more time, I would have written a shorter letter," though he may have stolen it from Blaise Pascal. "Je l'ai fait plus long que d'habitude parce que je n'ai pas eu le temps de le faire plus court."*]

One can only hope. [Regarding short stories.]

— Cecil Bothwell[3]
Asheville
"In the time of cholera"
The ides of May, 2021

*I have made this longer than usual because I have not had time to make it shorter.

2 There's a list a few pages back if you missed it.

3 Per Wikipedia®, Cecil Bothwell (born 16 October 1950) is an American politician, writer, artist, musician and builder.

Contents and Discontents

Sew True Cedes 13
Unyielding 17
Letting Go 20
Concession 24

Catch and Release 25
Flushing 29
Acquittance 34
Ellen Gives Up! 38

Demolition Derby 43
Failing That ... 48
Gurgitation 53
Deflated 56

Giving Up 62
Knot of Toads 67
Sweet Surrender 69
Getting Low 73

Relinquishing 77
Lost at Long Last 81
Confession 83
Sweet Surrender^2 88

Drain Flies Don't Bother Me 93
Expunge 94
Sneeze 97
Superceded 100

Mislaid 106
Degauss 108
Crestfallen 113
At a Loss 120

Throwing in the Towel 125
Lâcher prise 131
Giving In 138
Handing Off 143

(Discontents continued over leaf.)

~~Letting g~~...—No, *Really* Letting Go 148
Sans Gotch 153
Cashing In 159
Cashing In Again 163

Throwing in the Sponge 166
~~Erased~~ Toad Away 169
Erased 173
Deracinated 176

Shut Down 179
Cutting Loose 184
Crumbling 191, 105, 142, 158

Sew True Cedes[4]

I don't think there ever are. True ones, I mean. They're inherently reluctant. Anything ceded is, *ipso facto,* something that someone *didn't want to yield,* else it would be "gifted."

Does that make sense? What I'm driving at here is that if a person truly *gives something up* it suggests a heartfelt letting go, which one does with a gift but not a concession. A concession is extracted, like a tooth, and face it: No one goes into a serious dental procedure full of glee. (Well, maybe after nitrous?)

But here I've set myself up (see story title above) with the task of stitching together some sort of fictional quilt out of whole cloth regarding the up-giving of something or another. That's the name game I play, starting with a title for a book that forces my hand—or my pixels, I guess—demanding something like 200 pages devoted to thc beast thus conjured.

It's a difficult task, to be sure. But someone has to do it.

Truth be told, I don't honestly believe very many are *up to the job.* I mean to say, "I've been around the block a few times."

Here I'm throwing myself into the breach. Think of me as a sacrificial lamb fed raw to the ravenous muse of fiction.

Or, hey, a scapegoat. Whatever gets ceded from here on in? Blame me. I can handle it.

Or, well ... an Aztec virgin. Yes, that's it: Offering my beating authorial heart to the priest's razor-sharp obsidian knife for the good of the community. (And having mentioned Orwell ... 'nuff said. 'Nuff said.)

Now that we've settled the important matter of "with whom you are presently dealing," I believe we can proceed.

Franklin Franklin [and I think we have just learned a bit about this man's parents[5]] didn't see this thing coming and would have entirely escaped mention here if he were able. He were not. (Isn't that so very often the case? The embarrassment? Whooey!)

---

4 Influenced as ever by my immediate environment, when I started in on this collection I was gazing at a Sow True Seeds® catalog—a wonderful open-pollination, organic agro-vendor operation here in Asheville, which really doesn't deserve this kind of treatment. STS®? I apologize.

5 Really? Giving a kid that kind of name? What were they *thinking?*

Frankie[6] is a chestnut roaster during the holidays, with a little cart and an umbrella, parked outside of a pricey little health food store (which must charge him an arm and a leg for the privilege), wearing a fedora and looking all—whaddya-call-it?—European maybe? Like a storybook character, maybe out of Dickens or some German fairy tale?

What he does the rest of the year is anybody's guess—so yours is as good as mine. Go ahead. I certainly don't have time to play a silly guessing game like that this late in the day.

What we want to focus on here is what happened *yesterday,* smack in the middle of his annual chestnut vending *entreprise.*[7]

Yesterday was Boxing Day 2020 and, again, I'll leave it to you to explain the significance of *that* calendric coincidence. That it all came down on the most classically British of holidays is clearly one of those alignments that seems just "too-too." [So I guess we've settled on Dickens?]

You know? Of course you do.

Boxing Day was originally set up to give alms to the needy—one supposes by people feeling guilty about all the great stuff they ate, drank or gifted while the poor folk outside were clothed in rags, catching their death of cold or the plague, and starving—and so they boxed up the presents they didn't particularly like and re-gifted them to the destitute: Assuming, of course, that the original giftee didn't have the sales slip and so couldn't take the object back for a refund. [Charity often has that sort of double edge, methinks: Humans and humanity so easily diverge, though perhaps I'm being too harsh. The other side of this coin is that those of us who don't make enough to benefit from itemizing deductions on April 15th donate more to charity as a percentage of income, on average, than those who do.] [Fact.]

These days, obviously, it's the start of After Christmas Sales coupled with the After Christmas Returns Stampede, which also often requires boxing up of things: Misfit toys, ill-fitting sweaters, candy assortments unfit for consumption,[8] et. al.

---

6 And then to hang a child with this kind of hypocoristic? Really? Geeze.

7 Those unfamiliar with my vast literary output may not yet appreciate the way I introduce foreign words and phrases in order to attract the attention of judges for the National Book Award®. In this case, French. (Did you notice I used a Latin phrase in the very first graf? This little *évasion* is a class act, for certain.)

8 Maybe not those. Open boxes of candy invite deep suspicion. Or should.

But I can see by the way some of you are squirming around that you are impatient. "What, pray tell," you are thinking, "does this have to do with Frankie?"

Worms.

I guess you didn't see *that* coming!

Actually, *the lack thereof.*

(Or *that!*)

Terry Sommers has been an organic consumer for the longest time. We're talking decades here. She wasn't raised organic, of course—few were back then. But as a grown-up she mended her childhood ways and got religion.[9]

The thing about organic food, she'd tell you, isn't only a matter of what you put in your tummy, though it *is* about that.

"Never eat anything you can't readily pronounce!" she insists, and with that we can't reasonably argue. [Aspergillus Oryzae anyone?] [Castoreum?]

[Ha! Fooled you with that one! That's beaver anal gland juice! And it's a real thing, a food additive, and all natural! That is, assuming you regard terminating beavers with extreme prejudice to be "natural." Terry does not. By the way, it is said to have a "musky vanilla" taste that enhances fruit flavors. Yum?]

A dear friend was telling me two nights ago (yes, over Christmas dinner—thereby taking our lives in our hands, *not* social distancing in this time of cholera—though we've both been super-duper cautious regarding any other contacts—just so you know) about a visit to Montreal a few years ago, when she discovered that food products sold in Canada under the *same label* as food products on the shelf in U.S. stores didn't contain all the difficult to pronounce and clearly artificial ingredients routinely pumped into those of us dwelling south of the border.

Real food! Imagine that!

Well, Terry doesn't have to imagine what's in *her* feed bag. She eats natural products untainted by chemical addends, neither fertilizers nor insecticides, nor preservatives, nor industrial by-products—to whatever extent they are avoidable. Good clean food.

But, no, that's not the main reason why she gave up[10] on non-organic food. Her deeper concern was for the planet.[11]

The damage done via standard agriculture as practiced by

---

9 This is a metaphor. Terry is safely atheist.

10 Ceded, you see. And don't think she didn't miss Dove® bars at first.

11 Which concern recasts her decision as a gift. Fine line there.

inorganic farmers is immeasurable. Air, water and soil pollution is the inescapable result of modern agro-business. “We're killing the planet to feed ourselves,” is the way Terry would frame it, and, full disclosure, I agree completely. [Presumably why I mention it here.]*

Now, Terry bought a bag of chestnuts from Frankie last week. (Finally, you're thinking. Finally he gets back to the story.)

Yesterday she showed up with half the bag left over and asked for a full refund.

“What?” Frankie replied. “What?” He peered in the little sack. “They look perfectly good to me.”

“Not a worm in the bunch.”

“What? You want worms?”

“These aren't organic, are they *Mr. Franklin?”* (Emphasis hers.)

“Um ...”

“Am I right? *You told me they were organic. Your little sign claims they are organic.*[12]” (Again.)

Terry, I'm happy to report, got her refund and so wasn't forced into the uncomfortable position of having to picket a concessionaire on an 18 degree day.

Oh, Frankie. The nerve. The nerve. The nerve.

*This week, as I circled back for another edit [April 11, 2021] a phosphate mine full of water in Florida has posed a major threat to both downstream residents (had the dam burst) and Tampa ay as the excess water is pumped into the sea creating a very high risk of causing a red tide. Chemical fertilizer is full of surprises! Fun, fun, fun!

12 The nerve!

Unyielding

Right away my A-list readers are going to make the connection between "yielding" and "ceding." That is as it should be and offers us a very good place to start.

Tyrone Neibuhr[13] was dumfounded when he looked out his kitchen window on a crisp, snowy winter morning to see that his car was MIA. "How can that be?" he asked Tweed.

Tweed licked her paw but made no answer.

Ty hastened to his bedroom where he shed robe and slippers and donned more appropriate outdoor wear, then back downstairs to the kitchen and out the back door. A pair of skid marks ran all the way down the drive to where his Prius® was nosed out into the street. Freeze/thaw/freeze/thaw following yesterday's snow storm had apparently loosed the car's grasp on *sol gelé.*[14]

For you see, the ground was quite that.

"Lucky," Ty thought, and a pleasing thought it was. (Like most truly happy people, our protagonist entertains low expectations ("Expect the worst and you'll rarely be dis-appointed," is what Ty'd say.) And he was lucky indeed that friction exists.[15]

Absent that reductive interaction between tires and pavement, despite the icing—why, gosh, that Prius® would have t-boned Bob's Lexus®, parked, as it was, along the curb directly opposite Ty's auto.

This, quite naturally, turned Tyrone's thoughts toward questions regarding liability. Who would have held the bag in a case like that? *He* had been asleep. Could *he* have been held responsible for a wreck he had nothing to do with? Wouldn't that have been what is generally termed an Act of God?[16] If a neighbor

---

13 Naming characters is a tricky biz. In this case, a story about neighbors.

14 French again. Lofty *non?*

15 Note that like *Self-Evident,* (Brave Ulysses Books 2021), this is a work of friction: Gnashing of teeth and so forth.

16 Like all of my good characters, Tyrone is, of course, an atheist. But even atheists will use a figure of speech like this from time to time, particularly if dragged into court on a liability case.

kid like that Ralph Happler, who's always getting into mischief, had stolen the car and run it into the Lexus®, well that wouldn't be Ty's fault, would it? Nay, nay. Obviously not.

So if a “storm” “stole” a car, that would be the same?

Or would it have been Bob's fault? Putting his vehicle right *there* where mass attraction would inexorably draw two large objects together, as masses are wont to do. Wouldn't that have been contributory negligence? It was hardly Ty's doing that the local topography which necessitated his drive going *up* to his house dictated that Bob's go *down*.

Ty shook his head. Bob likely parked on the street when the storm was roaring in because last winter, after that humdinger of a blizzard, the Lexus® had been parked at the bottom of his drive and he hadn't made it up the hill for a week.

“Woulda been your fault, jerk,” Ty muttered. “Clearly.”

I think we get the feeling at this point that these across-the-street neighbors don't exactly get along. And we're right! Bob's a vehement proselytizer, and trust me on this, you don't want to let him get started. Just to be on the safe side I think we'd best leave him out of the rest of this story.

But what about Ralph? Is he really the sort of youngster who would steal a car? Is Tyrone being unreasonably judgmental?

It is a little bit of a stretch to imagine that just because someone has been caught egging and TP-ing homes, tormenting dogs and cats, saying bad words (though that line has surely been blurred by our unlamentedly former 45th prez) and otherwise behaving in a miscreant manner, he would be prone to grand theft. But as we learned upslope,[17] Ty has the happy habit of expecting the very worst from people, and is both rarely disappointed and nearly as rarely wrong.

What Ty can only surmise at this moment—and what will, in four short years, cause Bob[18] to visit the Happler household and pray with Ralph's parents, Nora and Phil—is what I'm about to make up.

At age 19 Ralph is actually going to steal a car! It's a snazzy little red Miata® and Belinda Fender is going to make the mistake of leaving the key in the ignition—in fact with the engine running (!)—because she had to go back in the house to get her grocery list—and Ralphie-boy will pounce on the opportunity.

---

17 You'll soon get used to the idea that, like a Prius® on an icy drive, all of my stories tend to run downhill.

18 I know. We were going to leave him out of this. But he's pretty pushy.

As Lindy comes back outside she'll hear the varooom! then watch her convertible sports car disappear around the corner! Yikes! He actually did it!

Nor can she immediately phone the cops since her purse *and cellphone* are in the Miata®! She'll have to run next door and see if Nora or Phil are home—not realizing that their son is the culprit.

They aren't, which may, in small part, explain why Ralph jumped the shark. Note that this idiom isn't usually applied to a situation like this, but I think it fits, or at least we can *make it fit*. The Urban Dictionary® defines it as "begun a downhill slide to mediocrity or oblivion." [Stay tuned.]

Then again, when you get right down to it, we're all on that well-traveled road. At least the oblivion part. But enough with profound musing—you're thinking, "What happens next?"

The second house over is Ty's, and he's home and happy to hand over his cell to Lindy, saying, "I bet it's that Happler kid."

After talking to the 911 dispatcher Lindy replies, "Oh, aren't you being a little hard on that boy?"

"Could be. We'll see." He pulls Lindy into an embrace and kisses her.[19] "We'll get this sorted out." He pats her bottom![20]

[She laughs, so we know she's OK with this.]

In just a brief 45 minutes or so a cop car pulls up in front of Lindy's home, ready to make immediate chase. (She's had time to dig around in her desk to find the tag number.) The officer asks questions and types responses into a laptop and in another half hour he barks into his cell: 10-5 dispatch, 10-31, we have a 10851, red Miata®, tag NC KILO FOXTROT ZULU 9274.

At this point Ralph has been on the interstate for well over an hour, traveling at speeds up to 90 mph. But he's almost out of gas, so he goes down an off-ramp, hits a patch of black ice, therefore fails to yield as he turns onto a state road and is T-boned by a 2021 Toyota Hilux Mako® pickup.

Jumped *by* a shark, I guess we'd have to agree.

Oblivion, indeed.

Given that most people seem to like the idea of staying alive this probably qualifies as a "cede."

---

19 This surprises us, but not Lindy for reasons which will shortly become obvious. And yes, this is Belinda Fender, the dentist we came to know and love in the wildly funny tale "In the Teeth of a Roaring Gale," in *Self- Evident: We Hold These Tooths,* Brave Ulysses Books, 2021.

20 Oh, the intimacy!

Letting Go

Well, that one was a little bleak. I don't usually knock off characters this early in a book, but when I learned that Ralph was the sort to torment dogs and cats ... well, no quarter given. Bad seed indeed and wasn't likely to lead to a bountiful yield. (The theft being four years in the future as of this writing, he still has time to mend his ways.)

On a cheerier note, and back to the present time, Tyrone and Lindy really hit it off and are well on their way to being itemized.

She was out for a winter walk and he'd just backed his Prius® out of the road. (It was way too slippery to get it all the way back up the drive.) They chatted, small talk since they'd not really gotten to know each other until this paragraph, placing large talk in the future, and he told her about the slip-n-slide.

"Can I join you?"

Lindy assented, and by the end of their hourlong stroll the two of them were feeling, um, "interested." I think that's the right word. (You have to start somewhere.)

Those of you (both?) who actually read *Self-Evident* are probably a little surprised just now. "Wasn't Lindy married? And now you're saying she's 'interested' in Tyrone? We thought all of your 'good eggs,' the ones who don't golf or much care for Dylan, didn't fool around! Shocked, we are. Really shocked!"

Now, now. You haven't let me tell you what they *talked about* on their walk. Calm down.

Ty, we can be pretty sure, and here I'll confirm it, is single. It's just him and Tweed these days. And friendly. He wasn't "hitting on" Lindy when he suggested the walk, he was just being neighborly and he enjoys a hike as much as you or me.

But what he didn't know until this very paragraph is that Lindy divorced Rob more than six months ago. I mean, if he were the snoopy sort who pays close attention to what the neighbors are up to he might have noticed the absence of Rob's ride. But he's not that type.

I mean, he *did* notice that someone bought the Miata. A red rag-top kind of stands out. But, actually, to the extent he'd thought about *that* at all, it seemed more like a mid-life guy thing.

But while Ty is un-snoopy, he's also perspicacious.

"Did he start golfing?"

"Yes. How'd you guess?"

"A lot of couples in Bothwell's books end up splitting over golf. Or Dylan. Happened to me."

"Yep. that too. I didn't know I was so typical."

"Consider the source."

So you see, before they permitted themselves to get "interested" they had determined their relational status. And by the time of the aforementioned vehicle heist they will have been lovers for more than three years. Hence the not unwelcome fanny pat, together with the hug and kiss. Comfortably intimate.

However, as noted on page 19, they will still live two doors apart, keeping a modicum of independence, chastened as they've been by prior personal histories.

Lindy is still in the dental biz,[21] numbing and drilling and filling, but we're completely in the dark about Tyrone, as was Lindy right up to now.

"I'm a day trader. Do it from home. That's why my car is parked here most of the time."

"Except when it decides to go sledding." She laughed.

"Right. And I just learned that you're a dentist.[22] Have you been in the trade long?"

"Seventeen years. Long, I think. But I still get a lot of satisfaction from it."

"Easing pain. Boy, there's nothing quite like a toothache."

"Yep. The industry's all about giving people a pretty smile, but pain is the thing. And, of course, death."

"Death?"

"Back in the day. In ancient Egypt. Killer bread."

"What? Bread? The Staff of Life?"

"All they had for grinding wheat was sandstone."

"Makes my teeth hurt just thinking about it."

"Wore the enamel off their molars. Infections went ballistic and killed a whole lot of Egyptians."

They walked in silence for a bit because that subject was kind of a buzz kill and here the idea was for them to "hit it off," though that phrase could take us into golf territory, which won't do. Not at all.

---

21 See footnote 19. Apparently Ty didn't read *Self-Evident.* Tsk.

22 Ibid.

Finally she said, "Trepaning."

"Come again?"

"Trepaning."

"I thought that's what you said. You trepan? Remind me not to switch dentists."

Lindy laughed again. "No. The Egyptians. They cut holes in people's heads with obsidian knives[23] to let the evil spirits out when the dental pain got too bad."

"Weren't they afraid they'd do serious damage?"

"They didn't think the brain had any importance. They believed all thinking and feeling was in the heart. I mean, they saved all the major organs in clay jars so a mummy could avail her or his self of necessary gear in the afterlife. But not the brain."

"Dentistry has come a long way."

"Mm-hmm."

"But I get it. About the heart. When Deb left my heart hurt something awful, despite the golf. We were in love back when. And I felt like I'd failed somehow. I mean, I bought her that first niblick,[24] back before I knew better."

"You shouldn't blame yourself. She could have ceded the habit before it drove a wedge between you.[25] I mean, if she'd loved you more than the game. Guess I was luckier, or dumber. I tried to make it work for the longest while, and by the time we split the heartache was past. A touch of nostalgia, sure. But what was past had passed."

"I got there too. After a while. Funny, the advice that struck home for me came from an actress. The woman who played Mary Ann on that silly sit-com, *Gilligan's Island*®. Dawn Wells.[26]"

"The cute one?"

"Right. She wrote a memoir, *What Would Mary Ann Do? A Guide to Life*. I don't know why I picked it up. I mean I'm not a person who much looks to movie stars for advice. But one thing

---

23 I'm beginning to think obsidian knives are going to be a *thing* here- though I made up the part about the obsidian vis-a-vis Egypt. I'm not sure Egypt has volcanoes. Sandstone, not lava. Sandstone knives?

24 Which I'll admit is fun to say. But a wedge-shaped club is virtually certain to drive a wedge between people if golf hasn't already wreaked.

25 See footnote 24.

26 Dawn Wells died of the Trumpidemic yesterday as I write this. I thought she deserved mention. She wrote the memoir with Steve Stinson in 2014.

really spoke to me. She wrote: 'Failure builds character. What matters is what you do after you fail.'"

"But you didn't fail. Deborah did."

"Well, that wasn't how it felt at the time."

"Glad it helped. But I'm not sure Wells' advice is entirely correct. Maybe '*can* build character' is more like it. Seems to me your ex, like mine, just kept on failing." Lindy snorted, "I mean, golf? Really? Is there a non-accomplishment more abject? Is there a deeper well awaiting a fumbling tumble?"

"I guess you got that right. Hey, would you like to join me for lunch? I love to cook."

"You're on. I don't. And I'm hungry. Maybe you can explain what a daytrader does while we're in the kitchen."

"By the way, I just discovered we have something important in common. You used the word 'game.'"

"How's that?"

"Golf is a game. It is definitely not a sport."

"You can say that again."

"Golf is a game. It is definitely not a sport."

[I think it's pretty clear at this point that they are apt to become very close—which, of course, we already knew based on that telltale fanny pat. Details matter, as do nouns.]

Concession

Is the dual meaning of that word not odd?

I'm glad you agree, or truth be told, I think we'd have to part ways right about now. I'm not sure I could live with myself if I discovered that *even one* of my readers was unperspicacious.

We saw that problem on page 16, did we not? We had Frankie Franklin running a concession, which he clearly wanted to do, and then *make* a concession which he clearly did not. It's enough to make your head spin.

It did his.

He lay awake that night, tossing and turning—as the idiom has it—much like the manner in which he rolled those chestnuts around on the grill *whilst*[27] roasting them, questioning his very *raison de vivre.*

Unfortunately—unfortunate because we genuinely wish he were a "good egg"—but, well, we can deal with it, because we (and I hope I speak for all of us here) are fortunate in embracing low expectations—he's not losing sleep over the fact that he lied about his chestnuts. Oh, if only. It could be a lesson learned. One of those profound embarrassments that help us see ourselves more clearly, thence to make amends. A mirror for the soul.

On that score he's feeling just fine.[28] In seven years of vending he's only been caught out once per the "organic" scripted on his little cart. And no surprise. Unlike the apples and oranges and whatnot inside the health food store where he sets up shop, chestnuts don't bear individual labels with the UPC code that tells a customer, "Eat me. I'm organic."[29] For that matter, if they did, they'd burn off during the roasting process.

No, Frankie's sleeplessness regards the forced concession from a concessionaire. "How," he wonders, "How do I square *that* circle?"

How indeed?

---

27 From British English. Hence the italics. A foreign word! Dickens!

28 A bad egg indeed. Golf is probably just around the corner.

29 The five digit code starting with 9-xxxx. Though, obviously, you still have to trust whomever put the sticker there.

Catch and Release

That gets one to thinking about fishing, naturally enough, and this story could definitely wander off in *that* direction—if I lose control, that is: Which, I hasten to add, I will not. I mean to say, a fisher-person[30] fly-fishing, say, on a dedicated catch and release stream who lands a really big trout is bound to be sorely tempted to take it home. Right? Particularly if said person forgot to bring a cell phone with which to snap a picture, or worse, pats a pocket and realizes that said cell has fallen into the rushing brook.

Bad enough to lose a six hundred dollar gadget, but to not have proof regarding the 25-inch-long brookie that had to go six pounds if it was an ounce? No one will ever believe (flipping a coin here ... heads, OK, male ... hoping that assigning "tails" to "female" doesn't seem sexist) him. Fred King's fishing buddies will just laugh. He can hear them already.

"Sure Freddie-boy. Sure. Where's the proof? You lost your phone too? Right, what's that in your pocket, a multimeter?"

"I bought a new one."

"Yeah, sure." And etc.

And he's correct. His fishing buddies are *that way*.

But before we move along to the actual story here, perhaps a pause to consider this whole idea of "catch-and-release" angling. The very notion is only possible in a wealthy society, a well fed culture. Fishing—a post-Neanderthal[31] "thing," by the way —was, and largely is, a matter of obtaining protein. The idea of spending, literally, thousands of dollars on a split-bamboo fly rod plus tackle, buying or tying ornate little imitation bugs, practicing and practicing the knack of laying out a long stretch of floating line with its monofilament leader, landing the aforementioned artificial insect just-so, in the quiet water below that boulder in order to fool a hungry fish ... thence to wrangle the misled critter into a landing net ... only to let it go?

---

30 Note how appropriately gender neutral I'm able to be. This makes me proud.

31 Neanderthals, as far as can be determined, did not eat fish. One of those facts that clutter my mental attic. Read more about that in the first chapter of *Whale Falls,* Brave Ulysses Books, 2010.

Really?

This is only remotely imaginable in a society where farm-raised salmon filets—and the pricier, allegedly "wild caught"—reside on beds of ice at the local supermarket, which is not to mention the millions of dollars spent on raising trout later loaded into tanker trucks to be dumped into streams for the entertainment of persons possessed of the above-mentioned equipment and inclination.

Is that nuts or what?

Anyway, now that I've pulled a new character out of the woodwork, and insofar as I only keep the admirable ones I manage to catch, we'll have Freddie sigh and slide the slippery monster back into the stream, thus establishing that he is a good egg and worth saving for some future fiction. That his whole enterprise seems a little bit stupid might be a subject for further discussion, but at least, within context, he is behaving ethically and adhering to the rules.

At bare minimum, he isn't golfing. So there's that. Furthermore, he is a fisher named King, which bodes. Oh it bodes, it does. It bodes. Geez, it bodes.

As indicated at the outset, I have no intention of traipsing off into a fish story at the present time. Whether that would be a good intention, hence a road to Hades, or a bad one—which, come to think of it, isn't much discussed in regard to pavement—is presumably not important, since I don't have it. Still ... hmm. If good intentions lead down, do bad ones lead up?

Maybe Billy Graham *is* in heaven.[32]

Shocked, I am shocked. [At the very notion.]

No, this story is about serious efforts regarding catching and releasing.

Giselda Magnon is a Realtor®. I know you're immediately going to leap to conclusions, but—trust me on this,—you're wrong. She's not like that at all.

The problem which just presented itself [to me—for her it is what we'd have to call a pre-existing condition] has to do with a rental house under her management. [See? You had her camped out on weekends in whatever home was open to the public at the moment, with a loaf of bread in the oven and fresh flowers on the

---

32 Note how cleverly I inserted a reference to the expired fraudster, granting me a plausible rationale to mention *The Prince of War: Billy Graham's Crusade for a Wholly Christian Empire,* BUB, 2007, 2009. As Billy used to say, "Untold is unsold!"

counter, which is not at all her shtick. She's a *property manager*.]

The Jacksons are off on a *grande tournée,*[33] as some people of means are wont to do. In a sailboat, no less. A very large sailboat. A craft. Actually ... a yacht! You'd be astonished. I am floored, simply imagining it. With a crew, no less!

Did you even guess that the Jacksons would attempt to circumnavigate the globe? Nor did I. But people you've only known for nine or ten sentences can be full of surprises.

And yes, they have a gun, not that they are "gun people." Piracy is sadly present and much more nasty than glamorous in these latter days. Blackbeard was so much more civilized.[34]

Which means the Jackson household is, or could have been, vacant. It may be true that "the rich are different," but like the rest of us, it surely tempts them to rent out a vacant property. In this particular case twelve thou a month will buy a lot of hard tack for the jolly Jackson crew, and so they employed Giselda to handle the details.

That rental price is meant to inform you—if the adventure on the high seas did not—that these folks "got rocks" as the saying goes.

She's a pro. I want you to know that from the get-go, so you'll see that what happened is not her fault. She screens people. Seriously screens. [Which, come to think of it, is why she's still single. And here you figured she was married. Right?]

Glenn Forster had "added up." Credit score, references, job info, driving a Beamer, first and last and damage deposit ... the whole nine yards. Everything *seemed* to be on the up and up.[35]

Until it wasn't.

The check didn't arrive. The phone calls weren't returned.

A knock drew no response.

Giselda peered in a window.

What? Or maybe: What!?

Vacant.

She dialed 911.

"I'm reporting a robbery. I need the police."

---

33 French!

34 See page 150 in the highly amusing *Fifty Wheys to Love Your Liver,* BUB, 2018.

35 Though the black eye-patch might have been a telltale sign. Maybe. On the other hand, one mustn't discriminate based on physical disability, even if the eye-patch wearer is faking it. Needing to appear disabled is itself a disability of a sort. Is it not?

She waited until the cops arrived to enter the house.

"What's missing, m'am?" Officer Jeff Hansen asked.

"Everything."

"What exactly do you mean?"

"Fridge, stove, dishwasher, microwave, kitchen table and chairs, a Mr. Coffee®, crystal wine glasses, silverware—and it's sterling, leather sofa and two chairs, coffee table, end tables, lamps, three beds—two queens and a king, four dressers, a desk and office chair, a computer—no, two, and a wifi router, miscellaneous chairs, a baby grand piano, a Picasso, two Renoirs," um, "I think two Van Goghs, but maybe three, and more art but I'll have to get a list at the office. Oh, and the bookshelf. Must have been a hundred books there. And the aquarium. Salt water. I think I have a list of the fish. Oh and the mounted moose head and the sailfish ... no, it's a swordfish, those were on the wall in the pool room. And the pool table! My god! How did he move that? And the sticks and balls and chalk. The toilet paper rolls? Really? And we haven't even checked the wine cellar."

"So some furniture and some paintings."

"Yes. Gracious me, I hope you ***catch*** him."

"Insured?"

"Of course."

"That makes things a little less urgent."

"What?"

"Just saying. What was he driving?"

"A BMW."

"That's a lot to fit in a trunk." [Which obviously makes no sense at all ... I'm just reporting what was actually said.]

So now the authorities are on the case.

And Giselda will have to ***re-lease*** the place. Not a pretty picture in her practiced view. "You should always rent a home furnished," is her rule. [Moving in and out is when most of the damage occurs in rentals.]

Meanwhile, we were worrying ourselves silly about the Jacksons in regard to piracy out there on Mother Ocean when the actual threat was right here at home.

There's a lesson in there somewhere.

(Beats me.)

Flushing

Kind of a combo of gifting and ceding, if you think about it that way—like the Beatles'® soap impression donated to the National Trust. But, really, don't go there. You'll end up like Freddie. You know, Freddie the fisher-person? [It's only been, what, five pages? Don't tell me you've forgotten already.] [Sigh.]

And not in the way you're thinking. Flushing has nothing to do with fishing,[36] outside of six shared letters, and very little to do with losing a cell phone. Damaging a cell phone, yes—and more common than you probably imagine—but not "losing" except perhaps in the context of functionality. Or, alternatively, in the sense of having totally, aquatically, "dropped the call."

Freddie, poor fellow—though not financially [I mean, do you *know* what plumbers charge these days? And how did you think he could afford a $3,000 split-bamboo fly rod, anyway?]—is given to mulling whilst he plumbs, plumbing the depths so to speak, in the course of righting the pipes.

He's inclined to ask the "Big Questions" *whilst* clearing the clogs and delaxating the leaks.

For starters—and here's one I bet you've dwelt on as well, knowing my readers as I do—"Why am I [is he] called a plumber rather than a pipewright? I (He) mean(s) just two paragraphs up, I [he] was credited with righting pipes and it isn't as if my [his] work involves lead anymore—it's all plastic and crimp rings and glue nowadays." So he is a pipewright, right? I think I'm not wrong.

"Plumbing," of course, owes its root to *plumbum,*[37] with all of its attendant "guilts by association."

"Flint, Michigan, anyone?"

Or, for that matter, the Fall of Rome?

Oh, I know the "experts" say that good old *plumbum*[38] didn't have *much* of anything to do with demise of the Empire, but, hey, Nero and Caligula were what are generally regarded as excessively wild and crazy guys.

---

36 At least, that is, now that straight piping has been mostly eliminated.

37 Latin again!

38 Ditto.

Freddie wants no part of them or that. Moreover, ontogeny is what it is.

Freddie sees himself as "still developing."

Just as the great and powerful Roman Empire chose to poison itself via leaden ducts, the great and powerful Fossil Fuel Empire chose to poison itself by adding lead to gasoline and dumping automotive waste into the Flint River. At least the Romans didn't know what was what. Pray explicate our excuse?

Freddie the Pipewright says [philosopher that he is] "Nuh-uh." The only times he's dealt with *plumbum*[39] is in its removal from old systems. He is, as we learned when he returned the big fish to the creek, a good egg. But wounded, nonetheless.

And said wound does not stop or even start with lead and its toxic discontents. He has reached and come up empty-handed, though not, of course, in his professional life. The hair clogs he has retrieved ... no, let's not go there, yuck—though some of them have been substantial enough to probably permit construction of an entire small pet, which might warrant mention. And slimy?

[Enough already!]

Rather, his emptiness regards purpose. Oh, not in pipe-righting, of course. That's practical, with obvious real world results, including a comfortable income (though, good egg that he is, our Freddie takes great satisfaction in fixing things for people who are really a little desperate.)

When the flush doesn't ... well, it isn't a pretty sight.

Nor, for that matter, in angling, also with obvious real-world results—though, as noted somewhere upslope, not exactly "practical" in catch-and-release situations.

Protein source? Not.

The purpose he seeks is notional and inclines him toward self-examination, singing along with Carrie Newcomer.

"Are you the pilgrim on the road?
Are you the hermit in the wood?
Have you followed what you know,
What you want or what you should?"[40]

---

39 Three uses of Latin in six short paragraphs. I believe this may be some sort of record.

40 John McGlynn, "The Fisher King," recorded by Carrie Newcomer on *The Gathering of Spirits* album, Philo, 2002

We see here—or, rather, hear here [hear hear!?]—the kind of questions Freddie asks himself, and no surprise! Not only is he inclined to plumb the depths,[41] he casts into them.[42] And for a man named King who angles, the song about, and more broadly the legend of, the Fisher King is apt to resonate.

Then, too, all of us—at least the thoughtful ones among us—have asked those questions, King or Belson or Ormond or Zelbecker or ... well, you know who you are. Have we followed what we know or wandered off into what we believe without proof? Have we lived up to the shoulds we embrace or yielded to wants we shouldn't have in the first place? We can't really argue for a better goal than to do what good we can, now, can we?

> "I am the wound that will not heal. I am the song you cannot sing
> I am the endless restless ache. I am, I am the fisher king
> And all that I can ask of you, is do what small good you can
> Speak the words that hear, and meet me where I am."[43]

You can see how that would bring out reflection in a man like Freddie. Or a woman. I mean, "a person like ..." *OK?*

Geez, you people.

Except that women, IMHO, are less often saddled with that particular wound. A fishing addiction is what it is, and there are far more men thus afflicted than those among the fairer sex. Perhaps, though this is only a guess, a person with a better developed sense of justice (and therefore, collaterally, injustice) is apt to take some exception to the whole notion of luring a being to its demise. Of baiting hooks—or baiting bears—for that matter.

Few women bait bears. You can take that to the bank.

The Fisher King [we're talking folklore now] was said to be the last monarch entrusted with possession of the Holy Grail in a time long before eBay®, which offers a swift solution to us, in this enlightened era, when possessed of something we'd rather not own. Nor Craigslist®. Poor man.

Not only that! He was "wounded in his thigh"—in the expurgated version of the fairy tale, that is—but unable to parent, which moves the wound somewhat north. And, get this, he was so weakened that all he could do was sit in a boat and fish!

This troubles Freddie, who, after considerable thought in

41 See third graf page 29.

42 Second graf page 25.

43 See footnote 40.

the course of replacing a broken clay pipe in the Proctor front lawn, dwelling on the deep meaning of the Fisher King story, muttered, "Nuh-uh."

Profound (if somewhat inarticulate) eh what?

That legendary King would only be healed when a noble knight arrived and asked the secret question, which it seems no knight knew, or at least no knight who knew the Fisher knew. Though it remains a possibility that the knights who knew were sadists and enjoyed tormenting the sad old man in a boat. [Note: "Good knights" sleep better. That's a fact.]

We know not all of the people in legends are good eggs. However, if you're like me, every time the idea of a "good egg" comes up I think of food. Not so much with "bad eggs." A good egg, boiled or fried, or poached and perched on a Thomas' English Muffin®? With Hollandaise? Yum!

Why, just last night Freddie was reading Thomas Wolfe and nodding in agreement: *"he had even then an intense faith in food, in housing, in comfort—he felt that a civilized man must begin with them; he knew that wherever the spirit had withered, it had not withered because of food and plumbing."*[44]

"Uh-huh," he'd mused, by way of agreement. The two went hand in hand.

As Nadine, the protagonist in the not to be overlooked story "Plumbing"[45] told her boyfriend, Martin, "It all comes down to plumbing." And while Martin guffawed, she was quite serious, though, in point of fact she was, and still is, a woodwright—a carpenter—for whom "plumbing" had a rather different and more structural meaning, depending as it did, and does, on a spirit level. Yet she too was, and is, a deep person, and included a breadth of meaning in her analysis: plumbing studs and jambs, plumbing supply and sewer systems and the very personal plumbing of mouth, throat, esophagus, stomach and so forth.

In fact, during that conversation pursuant to Martin's snarky "That's why they get forty-five bucks per hour,[46] Nade. Everything goes down the plumbing." [and I quote here]:

---

44 *Look Homeward, Angel: A Story of the Buried Life,* Thomas Wolfe, 1929, Chapter 11, fifteen grafs from bottom. Inclusion of this sort of *deep* quote is what the National Book Award® judges look for. *Non?*

45 The fourth story in the groundbreaking and hard-to-find *Can We Have Archaic and Idiot? 2,* BUB, 2009, 2018)

46 "Plumbing" was composed in about 1998, hence the low-ball estimate.

"Not what I mean and you know it." She chopsticked a bite of sushi into her personal pipes and added, "War, peace, here, there. Everything."

Well, I guess *she told him!* (Italics hers.)

Food and plumbing converged rather too closely in the matter of the Proctors' pipe break, in Freddie's view. Effluent had flooded out into the yard, revealing niblets.[47]

"Someone in the household doesn't chew," he mused.

Ewww! 'Nuf said.

Repair plumbing is for the strong of stomach.

But to climb back out of that gutter, let's circle back to Wolfe. I suspect most of us possess *" an intense faith in food, in housing, in comfort ..."* though some Buddhists I know claim otherwise, at least regarding the "comfort," not that I'm sure I entirely trust their claimed asceticism.[48]

Even those repeat offenders among us who circle back to the hoosegow on a tight orbit are said to appreciate "three hots and a cot." Housing, obviously, comes with the territory.

But here, it seems, we've wandered. So back to Freddie, singing along with Carrie.

"Just down the road and to the left
It's never been any further
To find the thing you never lost
who serves, who serves the grail."

"Uh-huh. 'S me. 'S what I'm after." Saith Freddie. "Fer sure."

---

47 Somewhat alliterative with "niblick," though for some reason not nearly as much fun to say. See footnote 24, page 22.

48 Just saying. From what I hear a lot of those weekend meditation retreats are pretty darn cushy.

Acquittance

A grudging cede, indeed.

You just know that a D.A. who has convicted an alleged criminal will be pretty darn upset when a higher court overturns that judgment. Dan Appler sure was. He was absolutely sure that Greta Strenberg had committed the crime with which she was charged and fully deserved the sentence meted out by Judge Laura Marsh Green, else he would not have prosecuted the case.

Appler is an honorable man, not the sort who suppresses evidence like that Kamala Harris woman in California. Give our Dan the DNA report and it goes right into the evidentiary record, and if that exonerates, so be it. Right is right and wrong is wrong, and you can quote him on that.

~~In this particular case DNA hadn't been a factor.~~

But what evidence there was regarding Strenberg and her alleged accomplice, Geoffrey Merced, seemed more than clear to Detectives Jim Pernal and Adam Gottsen, who had done the leg-work. Meanwhile Merced was still at large, meaning that Pernal and Gottsen were still on the case. Regular Sherlocks these two.

The pair had convinced Appler, who had fashioned an argument that convinced the whole jury: Dominic Hazelton, Hara Johnson, Fred King,[49] David Dwyer, Ellen Fulton, George Benbow, Melissa Tyner, Tyrone Neibuhr,[50] Dennis Vernon, Nadine Kershaw,[51] and William Bryce–if not Judge Green (about which more anon.)

The case seemed, as is sometimes said, "open and shut."

Finding the *Noblet*®[52] clarinet in Strenberg's Prius®

---

49 Yes, *that* Fred King.

50 Ditto, per Ty.

51 Yes, the carpenter. It's not like I have all day to come up with new characters, and jury duty is a civic responsibility.

52 Fun to say! Like niblet and niblick, though *Noblet*® is French, which makes it more important. And we are reminded that "niblick" is sadly drawn from golf. Which is *not a sport.* Meanwhile, you're going to get to read *Noblet*® five more times in the coming pages (seven in all, counting this footnote)—well on your way to fluency in a foreign tongue!

trunk, well, there you go! Isn't "possession 9/10 of the law?"

Yes and no. That phrase, clearly an over simplification, is normally used to indicate that if you're wearing a shirt there is an inclination to accept that it's *your* shirt—assuming it fits well and "becomes you," natch. If it's way too big, well, that's something else altogether. And if it's way too small, perhaps you are trying to show off well developed pecs or—what's the term I'm looking for here? A boob job?

The idea is that if it's *not* your shirt, then a claimant has a more difficult case to make than if, say, you weren't wearing it ... or something to that effect. If the glass slipper fits, etc.

But when it comes to an item that is in your keep that someone else has, say, the sales ticket for, and you do not? Well, well, you have some 'splainin' to do. And that was the case in this case in which the *Noblet* case and its contents were encased in the trunk of the Prius®, which we here note is registered to the accused. [Accused, convicted and now acquitted, no less.]

Whose *Noblet* is it, anyway?

There's the rub.

Cappy Thornsen insisted it was his, as his had gone missing.

It had gone missing, according to Thornsen's testimony, on the very night that Strenberg and Merced had attended a party at his house. Furthermore, both Alice Jensen and Larry Morris, fellow attendees of the funfest in question, had testified that there was a lively discussion about clarinets and their merits that night.

There had been a falling out, sad to say, and Merced and Thornsen had nearly come to blows over the matter of keypads and how often they ought to be replaced: annually vs. biennially.

The next morning Thornsen, set on his usual practice of playing the "licorice stick" from five a.m. to six—not a huge fave with the neighbors, given his level of mastery [low]—could not find his instrument!

He phoned the police and accused Merced of larceny. He also pointed to Strenberg as a possible crook.

Pernal and Gottsen couldn't locate Merced but they did find Strenberg, three days later, at her place of employ: Greenberg, Thompson, Lutz, Hunter & Phillips, LLC. [She had been clerking for those attorneys for many years, and they took her case pro bono.] The cops had a warrant and forced her to open the Prius® where they found *a*[53] clarinet.

---

53 Italicized here to indicate that we don't know yet if it is *the* clarinet.

Caught!

On went the cuffs. Poor Greta cried in the back seat all the way to the station—but she obviously knew enough to say nothing, and Delbert Hunter, Esq., arrived within minutes. Soon enough (meaning, hours of paperwork) she was out on bail.

During her trial she insisted that the *Noblet®* found in her trunk was *her Noblet®,* not Thornsens, and that she had been playing said instrument ever since high school.

Attorney Hunter even had her perform "Rhapsody in Blue" from the witness stand, as proof! [She is *very* talented.]

Oh, correction here. It now turns out this case *did* involve DNA, so scratch the fourth graf.

Attorney Hunter had the reed in said clarinet tested and the spit thereupon matched Strenberg's. However, Appler successfully argued that the fact that she had played it did not prove ownership.

I won't go into the intricacies of the prosecution and defense, but suffice it to say that while Greenberg, Thompson, Lutz, Hunter, Phillips and, obviously, Strenberg, believed in her innocence, Appler, Hazelton, Johnson, King, Dwyer, Fulton, Benbow, Tyner, Neibuhr, Vernon, Kershaw and Bryce did not. Jensen and Morris remained on the fence. Judge Green had to rule as the jury had decided.

Theft of an item worth $1,000 or less is a Class 1 misdemeanor in North Carolina, but Appler threw the book at Strenberg. If she'd pleaded out he would have given her the minimum: court costs, a small fine and one day behind bars, waived due to time served. (Four hours before she paid bail and was processed out.)

But she, and to be clear, her entire law firm, were *not having it.* She demanded a jury trial ... and as we've seen ... lost.

"Hold it, hold it," I hear you thinking, and thus imagine that you're going to raise an objection to the idea that all of this hoopla was over a misdemeanor.

But I'm wrong. What you're thinking is "Where is Merced in all this? Couldn't it be that *he* stole the clarinet and stashed it in Strenberg's car? Maybe she didn't know. What do we know about him other than that he's still on the lam?"

Good point.

[Though I'd hasten to note that the reed in the mouthpiece was shown to contain her DNA. So, she knew she had it, no matter whose *Noblet* it was.]

This brings us to the Appeals Court.

Merced knew he was a wanted man and was able to keep out of sight. Although he lives here, he works for a software company in Nevada, online, and his legal address is out west. He's about as low-profile as a person can get. His life is encrypted and block-chained out the yin-yang. He is also, I can assure you, a good egg. He was determined to help his girlfriend get out of her jam—though he's the cautious sort. No grandstanding. Well, not quite true. Grandstanding when it might serve a purpose, which you and I know it generally does not.

So he stayed on the down-low and did some sleuthing.

One morning, in the pre-dawn dark, not long after Greta's conviction, he had positioned himself outside Cappy Thornsen's house, when he heard the screech of a poorly tongued clarinet. He crept to a window and cautiously peered inside.

Thornsen was tootling. A *Noblet®!*

How? What? Oh my! [The other being held as evidence.]

He pounded on the door.

Thornsen, assuming it was one of his complainant neighbors, shouted, "I've got every right to play music in my own home!"

Merced pounded again.

Nothing.

The door was unlocked. He went in.

"What's that in your mouth, buddy boy?"

Thornsen paled. "Um."

"You had it the whole time, right?

"Um."

"And you let Greta get sent up, to the Big House for a full half-day! You bastard!"

"Time served. She didn't actually ..."

"Tell it to the judge, mister."

Which he did when the case was remanded to the lower court.

Judge Green: "Can you explain to the court?"

"I told the truth. I couldn't find the *Noblet®* the next morning."

"And."

"I couldn't find it for over a week."

"And."

"It was under the sofa."[54]

---

54 Anticlimax at its finest! Now you are probably thinking this whole affair

Ellen Gives Up!

See! We've already found a place in our hearts and on this page for Ellen Fulton. We didn't really get to know her during jury deliberation—which, after all, was behind closed doors and only took fifteen minutes. About the only facts we know in her regard are first and last names and that she, like all the other jurors, was mistaken when she bought the prosecution's viewpoint.

Mistakes happen and here's the thing—when the truth emerged she was not only remorseful but sent a nice card to the Strenberg woman. That tells me she's an empath.

But she doesn't wear that on her sleeve, else she'd never have been picked for jury duty. A prosecuting attorney generally doesn't want someone who might feel sympathetic to the accused, the inverse obviously being the rule for a defender.

As it happened, in the heat of more than an hour of courtroom drama, and despite the fact that Thornsen was and is kind of a jerk—and, frankly, seemed so on the stand—Ellen's kind thoughtfulness kicked in. She felt sorry for a young man deprived of his beloved woodwind. This, she thought, could have been her son who had struggled to learn to play the ukulele only to have lent it to a friend who set it on fire.

[Tony claimed it was an accident. A likely story.]

When Delbert Hunter, Esq., had questioned her, during jury selection, one of his standard queries was, "Have you or any members of your immediate family ever been victimized by a thief?"

She had honestly answered in the negative. Tony Glintz hadn't *stolen* the ukulele, after all. Donnie had ceded it, willingly. That Tony was a firebug[55] wasn't exactly clear at the time. [Ultimately the ukulele would prove to be just the start of a fiery

---

looks pretty pointless. But no. I have used this break from composition of high-quality fiction to introduce nineteen new characters! I am *so* ready for what's to come!

55 Which reminds us, does it not, of the arsonist/firefighter Elmore Stringfellow, who appeared twice in *Self-Evident: We Hold These Tooths,* BUB, 2021. Admittedly a bad egg.

career.[56]]

The story of the flaming uke isn't really part of what I'm about to tell you about Ellen other than, perhaps, to let you know that she's a mother and the mother of a creatively gifted young man.

How many kids take up a serious musical instrument at age seven? Moreover, he was already good! You'd think he'd been born with a lei around his neck in the shadow of Mauna Kea with a Mona Loa® macadamia in his mouth.[57]

A prodigy in the making, all gone up in smoke.

Little Donnie took it as a "sign" that the uke wasn't meant to be his instrument and asked Santa for an *electric* sitar. Ellen and Don, Sr., were a little surprised, of course. They hadn't even known there was such a thing.

[Full disclosure: Neither had I until I went online just now to find out how much a sitar costs. My knowledge of the instrument was kind limited to images of Ravi Shankar® wrapped around a gourd with a long neck bearing 18-21 strings, which, honestly, seems a far cry from a ukulele. However I learned that the electric sitar has ly onsix strings, just two more than a uke, and thus is well within the grasp of, now, eight-year-old fingers.]

[Further full disclosure: In the paragraph about the Santa request I originally had Little Donnie ask for a plain old sitar, but went back and added the "*electric*" after my investigative browse.]

The folks were surprised, yes, and a little taken aback. I mean the ukulele had cost about $25, and a low-end electric sitar was going to set them back more like $500. Kind of a jump for a thing that might just be a passing whim on the part of a youngster. A rising third-grader can have a lot of notions.

Ellen had told her husband, "He's talented, but isn't that kind of pricey?"

"We can probably find a used one for a little less. There are some listed on eBay®."

"Well, true."

"And if he loses interest, we can resell it later."

"As long as he doesn't loan it to that Glintz kid."

Don laughed. "Hope he's learned his lesson there."

That, of course, is not what this story's actually about. But

56 Though not as a firefighter. Some firefighters are arsonists, but, contrary to popular opinion, not *all* arsonists are firefighters.

57 This is my Hawaiianized version of "silver spoon."

it is unusual enough for a child that young to ask for a musical instrument so far out of the ordinary that I thought it bore mentioning.

"What," you've been wondering for two full pages, "Did Ellen give up?"

Let me think.

It has to be something fairly significant or why, pray tell, would it warrant title status? Titles matter, generally speaking, though that couple formerly known as Royals, who moved stateside to burnish their fortune as versus their status, seemed not so taken with royalty. [Face it, the Crown's wealth is mostly on paper and in drafty old castles. Sure, you've got the gemstones, but it isn't like you can sell them. Meanwhile you're basically living on the dole, determined by the whim of Parliament.]

One supposes being an heir to a throne is less alluring in this era of prolonged old age—Prince Charles being the poster child of that dreary doom.[58] Back in the "good old days" kings and queens blinked off at a pretty good clip, and being even third or fourth in line for the crown wasn't clearly a "dead-end" job. Rather, sitting in the throne itself was often a short ride to an unhappy ending, the wives of King Henry VIII being the poster-girls for that gloamy gloom.

You've really got to think that one of them would have found opportunity to diddle some lusty commoner and make Henry a son, haven't you? (Ann Boleyn gave it a shot.) When he was off hunting roe deer or something, hoeing your own row, so to speak. Then, to keep the secret safe, you could easily have the lusty commoner's head on a platter, or a pike, and none would be the wiser. I mean, think about it, even if you liked the fellow, even enjoyed the tryst, and therefore, being of the fair sex[59] did not call for decapitation, what are the chances yon lusty commoner would squeal?

A chopped-off head is much to be preferred over what an angered king might have pulled off. Arms and legs wouldn't be the half of it.

But getting back to Ellen, it has to be something meaningful. Ah, I have it! This is a good one.

Ever since little Ellie was about the same age as the

58 Not to mention the fact that there's serious talk about winding down the whole shtick after QE2 moves on, the whole affair having become more soap opera than "ruling family" these days.

59 See page 31 in re: Women and justice.

budding sitarist, Don Jr., she has had a somewhat secret goal. His creativity had to come from somewhere, after all. [And Don Sr. is, well—not to put too fine a point on it—kind of dull in the art department, which is not to say he ain't a great guy.] She hasn't even shared it with him. When she finally succeeds will be the time for that. "Ta-da!" she'll proudly exclaim.

So she's worked on her project alone and under wraps. Don is out of town a couple of days a month, visiting the main office in Atlanta, so she can easily engage in the effort in his absence, meaning that early failures, so often the practical outcome while crawling up a learning curve, don't have to lead to marital embarrassment.

As we discussed at fairly extensive length in *Self-Evident,* everybody lies about things great and small, often telling ourselves we are sparing others, but more often sparing *nous-mémes.*[60] We want the esteem of others because it helps us feel good about *nosotras mismas.*[61] And, like it or not, it is probably never more crucial than between intimate friends or matrimonial partners.

Lies grease the wheels of love, but, to get back on track here, shortening greases the "wheel" of a bundt pan.

Yes, ever since little Ellie was actually little she has dreamed of baking a perfect angel food cake, just like her Grannie Eleanor. Eleanor was a baker's baker, and the sponge cakes she pulled from the oven (with little Ellie's "help") were perfect every time.

They were spongy and delicately browned, absolutely delicious with strawberries and whipped cream, or chocolate icing, or Princess Anne cherries and juice. The memories! Oh the memories!

Ellen has so wanted to create the selfsame fond remembrances for her son, and to present Don Sr. with that *fait accompli.*[62]

She has gone to extraordinary lengths to mask her consistent failure. I mean, they *all fall,* every one, while cooling. She just can't seem to get it right. [Maybe the elevation?]

So as soon as Don heads off to the big city, she hurries to the store for ingredients—and (here's where it gets extraordinary)

---

60 Told in French in order to avoid repeating the word "ourselves" twice in one sentence. I hope those judges are paying attention!

61 Ditto, only in Spanish!

62 *Hecho consumado* in Madrid.

—an angel food cake from a bakery. This way she's ready in case of what has come to be a dismal track record.

She has even gone so far as to intimate that the store-bought ones with which she greets Don each month are of her own creation. Not verbatim exactly. What she does is pour on the selected topping and say, “I made this for you, darling.”

But subterfuge is a slippery slope and, like any infidelity, subject to discovery when routine is disrupted. Which, I'm sorry to report, happened yesterday.

Don came home *a day early*. While the latest attempt was in the oven.

“Something smells good honey!” were the first words out of his mouth.

“Oh, you're home!”

He put his arms around her and kissed her, genuinely glad to be back in their happy domicile.

“What you cooking?”

“A surprise.”

He went into the kitchen for a glass of water and spied the unboxed cake on the counter. “Oh, angel food. I love your angel food cakes honey.” He peeked in the oven. “Oh, two?”

She nodded.

The one in the oven fell, as usual, once it was out.

“I give up,” she muttered to herself, feeling profound remorse. As we noted *in re*[63] the trial, she is an empath and now feels enormous sympathy for herself.

“I totally give up.”

I suggested she might want to stick with brownies out of a box. Almost everyone[64] likes brownies better than sponge cake anyway, and dollars to donuts that's true of Don.

---

63 Latin again! On a roll!

64 See footnote ~~156~~. ~~157~~. ~~158~~. 159. (Am retaining earlier numeric iterations of this footnote in order to offer a window into the creative process.)

Demolition Derby

It's inherent. When a man (and, trust me, it's almost certain to be a man) enters his auto in an exhilarating afternoon or evening of mechanical destruction, he has given up. At least on the car, and perhaps on everything. Desperate much? Perhaps.

True, there are rules intended to protect the drivers. All glass removed, no T-boning and, most critically, always and ever in reverse, the point being, principally, to smash the radiators of other contestants, leading inexorably to overheating and mechanical failure.

What fun!

[Full disclosure: A “friend” almost persuaded *me* to drive *his* decrepit car in one such, but we were saved by two clear-thinking women. One, his wife, who convinced him that there actually remained some cash value in the thing. The other, my girlfriend, who convinced me that it was an incredibly stupid idea. In my defense: I was not yet 30. Brain barely fully formed.]

Not so for Dennis Vernon, and this ... what should we call it? Poor judgment? ... I think that fits ... surely helps to explain his vote on that jury. The '73 Ford LTD® in question was definitely on its last legs or, more properly, wheels, burning oil like a furnace, gears grinding, tie rods so worn they were about to fall off. Brakes? Metal on metal. Not, we can be certain, street-legal.

His line of reasoning, to the extent that the term applies, involved the prize money. A cool thousand to the last operational vehicle and half that to the runner up. On top of that, the decision involved a woman, Hara Johnson.

Yes they'd only met ten pages ago, sitting on that jury, but they had clicked. They're now marginally itemized,[65] though not cohabiting, FYI. Yet, anyway, we'll see.

S they're still at that stage where he's trying very hard to impress Hara, and risking life and limb in such a mortal (to metal) combat seems like just the thing to prove his derring-do.

Nor did she demure.[66]

---

65 Perhaps leading us to question her judgment.

66 Confirming her thoughtlessness—assuming, of course, that her interest in Denny is sincere. I mean, if they were married … life insurance?

In the week before the Big Day, Denny removed the windshields, front and rear—carefully to be sure. (They are probably more valuable than the rest of the car put together. Ditto with the lights and the spare.) Then he borrowed a truck and a trailer from his best friend, though this raises the question of what kind of friend would abet such a foolhardy enterprise.

Jim shook his head but said nothing.

Our daring young man arrived at the track early, in plenty of time for the requisite registration and inspection. The $75 entry fee, he knew, was simply a down payment on his eagerly anticipated grand prize, plus, naturally enough, the $100 security deposit required to ensure that contestants would haul off their own wrecks after the joust.

Hara, of course, drove separately, since Denny suggested that she needn't deal with all the rigamarole ahead of the Big Event. Truth be told, though she hadn't elected to talk her man out of his plan, she *was* somewhat worried about him, and drank a large pitcher of *piñas coladas*[67] in the hours leading up to the show. [She ought not have driven, IMHO.]

The demo derby was the evening's last event, a scheduling necessity since the track would require extensive cleanup after the fact. Denny sat with his lady-love during all of the races, watching the souped-up stock cars racing round and round, "trading paint" as the regulars called it. He had the piss-willies, jiggling a leg the whole time, anticipating his coming triumph.

Hara was giggly and in high spirits, practically devouring him with kisses, making kind of a drunken spectacle of herself. But she was too over-the-top to care, and he was so distracted by his calculation regarding the pending smash-up that he enjoyed her ministrations somewhat less than he otherwise might.

As the final race screamed to its clamorous conclusion, Denny accepted one last kiss for good luck and proceeded to the yard where his chariot awaited.

The announcer introduced the contestants with great fanfare: drivers' names, car models and years, together with rules and, finally, the prize money. Then, "Gentlemen, start your engines—if they will start! Ha-ha!"

From a raised platform beside the track another fellow fired a starting gun, and the *mêlée*[68] was on.

Denny's *secret strategy* was to avoid conflict at first,

67 Spanish!

68 French!

backing around and around but never going stern to nose with the other competitors. Of course, that was the “secret strategy” of all of the 14 drivers. [In order to prompt action the rules included a twenty minute time limit. If a winner didn't emerge in that span, no one would claim the prize.]

The cars roared rearward in circles as the digital clock on the scoreboard counted down. With each tick of that timepiece the pressure built. Who would make the first serious move?

Suddenly the black Chevy Impala®, I think a '79, veered toward Denny's grill and he blasted away just moments before any serious damage was sustained, though even that slam-bang of bumpers jolted him.

Now a pale blue Dodge Aspen®, might be a '76, slammed into the black Chevy® whose driver had been looking back at Denny as he geared up for another attempt. The impact was solid and the water, then steam, pouring out of the Impala®, signaled looming death. The crowd roared!

[Note: Telling this as a sequence belies the action, which rapidly became an “all at once” sort of thing.]

A green Pontiac GTO®, maybe early '70s, too rusted to be worth restoring, slammed into a yellow Chrysler Newport®, I think early '80s, but I could be wrong, while a brown Chrysler Cordoba, had to be a '76, mashed the Aspen, tearing off the right front fender, as Denny took aim at the GTO® and a grey-blue Mercury Monarch®, pretty sure a '75, took a hit from a dark green Buick Century®, couldn't be newer than '81. [I think we're up to eight models, and honestly, they're moving around so fast I can't keep up with what's hitting what. I believe you get the picture. Mayhem! Total mayhem!]

Seven have now met their matches, leaving the infield cluttered with obstacles to the remaining half, as they chase one another around and between the steaming heaps. While this is an exhilarating brouhaha for the live audience in the stands, I can see that it's kind of weak tea on paper, so rather than continuing with the whole sequence of what did what to whhic, I'll just jump ahead. If you want more excitement you can re-read the previous graf. Really, several times if that floats your boat or shifts your gears.

So now we're down to three and Denny's still in the mix! One rear quarter panel is dragging, but it hasn't hit his tire yet. Rather than come up with more car names, and in the interest of moving things along, we'll decide that the Century® and the, hmm, flipping a coin here, OK ... the Monarch® are still rolling, though they too have fenders bent and crumpled.

Hara, by the way, is screaming herself hoarse. "Go Denny! Go! Go! Go!" If he could hear her he'd be pleased, but in the roar and clamor the drivers hear nothing but internal combustion and the rending of metal.

The three survivors have moved into the clearest part of the track as the scoreboard ticks past four minutes. It's imperative that they make their moves. Denny is in hot pursuit of the Monarch®, which is making for the Century®. That embattled vehicle takes a solid on the front left quarter, which spins the Buick® just as the driver guns it to get away, hence races backward into Denny's driver-side door. It's mashed way in!

A T-bone! Not intentional—true—but illegal nonetheless. The announcer, who owns a half interest in the track and recognizes a profitable opportunity when it presents itself, wants to call an end to the festivities. No winner, no prizes. On the other hand, he knows the crowd would be furious if he stopped it now. What to do?

But what's this? Who's that racing across the infield? Why, it's Hara! "Denny! Denny honey! Are you OK?"

The announcer pounds on the emergency button, sounding a klaxon and lighting up the flashing red emergency lights. The show is over. Denny is furious.

The crowd is divided between booing and awing. Aw, she loves him so much! Boo! Run her over if she's that stupid!

"Why did you do that?"

"Honey, I was worried!"

"But I was going to win!"

"I'd rather have you alive!" (Aw, gee.)

A track official took Hara by the arm. "Come along. You can't be on the field."

The boos increase. Now they're stomping on the grandstand, in unison. Clomp. Clomp. Clomp.

The announcer is befuddled. The fans are regulars. He can't disappoint them. Three cars are still running.

"Damn it!" (This to himself.) Then, over the speakers, "Tom Delancey, in the Buick Century®, is disqualified for the T-bone." (A few boos erupt from Delancey's backers.) "We'll restart the clock at three minutes. Three, two, one." With that he doused the red lights and flashed the greens. Onlookers roared their approval.

The two remaining cars circled and dodged, lunging. There was no chance of either taking a radiator blow at this point —no way to line up and jam—so crushing a fender became the goal, aimed at flattening tires. They nipped at each other, desperate now as the clock wound down, knowing that absent a win by one, there would be a win by neither.

Which somehow suddenly clicked in Denny's mind. The only way to win, at this point, was to lose. Every ounce of testosterone in his body ... [That can't be right, can it? So I looked it up. He is of average build, and he's about 30 years old, so he has approximately 1.7636980974789998 ounces of testosterone in his bloodstream ... meaning it is plural ... "ounces" ... meaning that the "every ounce" is an appropriate referent ... OK, back to the story.]

Every ounce of testosterone in his veins is telling him he must be the winner! (*Le gagnont!*) (*El ganador!*) (ο νικητής!)[69]

But, surprise! He's just realized that he can get the $500 if he cedes. He turns face on to his rival with just moments to spare. The driver of the Mercury® seizes his chance and races full tilt, slamming into the Ford® with his right rear quarter, crashing deep into the other's radiator. A huge cloud of steam envelops the scene as Denny's motor sputters and dies and the Monarch® takes a victory lap around the track, now in forward gear, wheezing and careening but still very much alive.

The grandstand goes wild with cheers and whistles and hoots as the winner limps by. The announcer sighs, but realizes that $1,500 lost will come around in the end, and announces the winners.

The wrecks are towed from the field and loaded on trailers for those who are hauling their own to the scrap yard, or into a back lot for those who'd rather pay the hundred bucks. Once loaded, Denny heads for home, grinning to himself at the way he snatched a partial victory from certain defeat. She is going to be *so* impressed at his smarts!

His cell phone rings. It's Hara!

"Hi honey! I picked up five hundred!" ($425 net.)

"Don't honey me."

"Baby, whatsa matter?"

"You threw it, mister. You blew it." With that she hung up.

What profiteth it a man to win five Big Bens if he loseth the girl when he giveth up the game? A lesson for our times.

69 Here we've added Greek!

Failing That ...

So here I've been telling you about Denny and Hara, for whom you really felt no particular affinity, while all along you've been dying to get to know George Benbow. I get it. Denny is kind of a loser, except of course that he won by giving up—won one thing, that is, while losing Hara—which is kind of "Buddhist" when you get right down to it.

He discovered his Buddha-nature in the nick of time, is one way to look at it, though, obviously, Gautama would likely suggest that letting go of one's ego is not supposed to be a paid proposition. Enlightenment should be its own reward absent enrichment, though, truth be told, enrichment of, say, uranium, can lead to a very bright light indeed.

Boom!

Hara comes off as the less enlightened but more ethical of that former pair. Contests are not to be *thrown* (italics hers.) It goes against the whole idea of competition, and she wants a partner who'll carry her scarf into the joust and win.

Or die trying.

Want is the problem. She still wants. When she finally finds *prajna* she will no longer want, though that will take her to the next problem: "How do I decide what to do if I don't *want* to do anything?" (And more about her "wants" anon.)

As Bucky Fuller used to quip (paraphrasing now): "The beauty of solving a problem is that it leads one to the next, more difficult problem." For Bucky the world was an endless series of Russian dolls, I suppose, but stuck together in such a way that getting to the next one was no simple task. Regular matryoshkas are actually only fun the first time through, which is why I never answer those e-mails titled FindRussianLady. Just saying.

For some reason all this exploration of Buddhism, which I think is important in and of itself, reminds me of the old saw about *Siddhārtha Gautama's*[70] pizza party. He only ordered three large ones for his guests of whom there were at least two dozen.

---

70 This is the same in French and English, but सिद्धार्थ गौतम in Hindi! Isn't language fun?

At the end of the evening his disciples were crying out, "Piece! Piece! But there was no piece." Next time he should be more mindful, IMHO.

But you were asking about George, weren't you?

Well, for one thing, George has never considered entering, or even attending, a demolition derby. That says worlds. To go a step further, he's avoided attendance *or* participation without any input from the fair sex, which puts him one up on yours truly.[71]

This isn't to suggest that he's never done anything truly stupid, but I think we should give credit where due. Furthermore, it probably bears mentioning that he's unlikely to ever own a car that would be a candidate for such an excursion. He's very attentive to maintenance regarding his ride: Fluids, tire pressure, wash and wax—the whole nine yards. He vacuums weekly.

Which makes what I'm going to tell you now an enormous surprise. *Ginormous,* really.

Some years ago, almost 40 as we speak, George took a job on the construction site of the Seabrook Station®, a nuclear power plant on the New Hampshire coast.[72]

I'm guessing most of you know that construction of a nuke involves a whole lot of concrete. Megatons. Mega mega. What some of you may not appreciate is that, in order for concrete to reach its full strength, it must be kept above freezing, preferably above, say, 40 degrees Fahrenheit (4.44444°C, for those of you living in more scientifically enlightened lands) until it is well-cured.[73]

I would suppose that most of you entertain a sturdy preference for nukes built to spec, not that I *in any way* assume that *any* of my readers actually "prefer" nukes, given that they are too expensive to operate absent government subsidy and have created a waste problem for which there is no solution in the foreseeable future.

As energy geek Amory Lovins once observed, "Producing electricity with nuclear power is like cutting butter with a chain saw."

But setting that aside for the purpose of argument: I think

71 See page 43 if you skipped ahead.

72 I know some of you have been puzzling over my mention of uranium on the previous page, but really? Here you are, already a quarter of the way to the Book Club Study Questions, and I'd like to believe that I've established the fact that I know what I'm doing here.

73 I feel certain this will come in handy for my DIY readers.

we can agree that if there is going to be a fission plant in the neighborhood, we'd be more comfortable if the thing was built to last—though "last" might be problematic. Fukushima is leaking like crazy nine years after the tsunami, pouring radioactive water into the Pacific, while the interior of the reactor is beyond repair. It's so radioactive that humans spending more that about ten minutes inside would receive a fatal dose.

This will continue for approximately 250,000 years, which presents what we might call a "line item" problem for the Japanese National Diet.[74]

When we think of safeguarding something for a very long time, our thoughts naturally turn to Egypt. Those pyramids were built to last! The oldest are around 5,000 years old! Whooey!

So maybe we should stuff radioactive waste into pyramids? They seem to shed water pretty well, and the Pharoahs set a great example in that when they died all of their servants were killed and buried with them—given that the boss would need servants in the afterlife.[75]

So we could hire a bunch of deeply religious people who are convinced that there is a heaven, and pay them a lot of money to haul the waste into the pyramid, and then bury them with the stuff. See? And while the Great Pyramid required an estimated work force of 20,000 over a period of about twenty years, we have power equipment and could probably do it faster and with fewer worker bees.

The main problem I see involves the "No Trespassing" signs. Here we are, a brief 5,000 years on, and I'll bet you five dollars you can't read it in Greek (Χωρίς καταπάτηση), let alone in hieroglyphics. If there are any of our heirs and assigns running around here in 250,000 years I kind of doubt they'll be fluent in English, French, Spanish, Russian, Chinese, Hindi, Urdu, and so on and so forth.

Looking back that far we see the first appearance of *Homo neanderthalensis,*[76] generally assumed to be kind of weak in the foreign language department. To be fair, it has been discovered that modern humans have a bit of Neanderthal DNA in their double helices, so presumably those cave people were able to pitch a little woo. Furthermore recent research has confirmed

74 As distinct from the Japanese national diet, which presumably includes irradiated fish at present.

75 They were nothing if not practical.

76 More Latin! This is so cool!

that Neanderthals were making shell jewelry at least 45,000 years before we moderns figured that out, which means they had a serious head start on impressing their dates with necklaces and other baubles. Limpets may not be a girl's best friend, but they had to be a step up from "no jewelry at all."[77]

Bling is in the eye of the beholder.

Additionally we now know that Neanderthals were doing cave paintings 24,000 years before our forebears. Inviting someone over to see one's "etchings" has a storied history vis-a-vis seduction, and philologists believe that anyone who paints images necessarily has language skills because symbolism implies thought: i.e. "A picture paints a thousand words," though the sample of Neanderthal art lately depicted in a *NYT*® article looks like a badly constructed ladder. Caves are inside rock formations, and thus don't need roof repairs. So a ladder? Dunno.

I know, I know, we could post signs with skulls and crossbones that sort of suggest a threat, but at the present rate of proselytization it isn't unlikely that the post-*sapiens sapiens* in that high and far off time, as Kipling called such, will all be devotees of the Flying Spaghetti Monster—whose devotees, we well recall from our reading of *Seize You on the Dark Side of the Moo,*[78] believe the FSM first created pirates, from whom we are all descended. (We share 99.8% of our DNA with pirates! Much more than with, say, chimpanzees. Case closed.)

Such devotees are apt to think the pyramid behind the sign is a relic of The Creation and dig right in, with lamentable results.

And, duly noted: Even a few thousand years along, the pyramids were robbed of their loot, long before we bright lights had any clue what the hieroglyphs meant. The Rosetta stone wasn't even discovered until 1791, much less deciphered.

But I digress.

We were talking about George's job, performed during the first term of that old rascal Ronald Reagan—and boy oh boy, did Ronnie screw the pooch, or what? Things were going kind of OK under Jimmy Carter: Balanced budget. Solar panels on the White

77 I'm not going out on a limb here. According to Alexander Stoessel, an evolutionary biologist at Friedrich Schiller University Jena in Germany who studies acoustic communication, "They had sex with each other, so some kind of communication was probably likely." (CNN® 3/1/21) Not so sure about that, considering some couples I've known.

78 BUB, 2019. You *have* read it, right?

House roof. Sort of a Mr. Rogers® presidency. Ah, well.

Because George had some years of experience as a masonry foreman, he was hired to oversee the heating of the enclosed space where concrete was being poured. They tented each area with polyethylene, something like a hoop-type greenhouse, and fired up the salamanders. [These were kerosene-fueled heaters with powerful fans. But more about actual "salamanders" on page 139.] Thermometers were placed at critical locations throughout the job site—this before the Blue Tooth® era—which then required documentation. George was to make the rounds during his shifts (twelve hours per day, with his assistant covering nights—both cleaning up on O.T.!)

We were pretty good friends, and one day I asked him how he managed to keep the temperature up in midwinter. New Hampshire, after all, is cold as can be. Sometimes it was double digits below zero.

His answer: "Aw, Cecil. It's just paperwork."[79]

In fairness, I ought to add that he added. "I tried. I really tried. But it was impossible. So I gave up."

79 I "sincerely regret to inform you" that George was a real person named George, though I've changed his last name, and he really held that job, and he really told me that. This is at least part of the reason I moved 959 miles south and west. You can't be too careful.

The phrase "sincerely regret to inform you" always rockets me back to Frank Zappa and The Mothers of Invention® album *Burnt Weenie Sandwich.* But that's just me. And, of course, that phrase harkens back to the nice notes sent by the military to families whose lads were cut down in Vietnam. "Greetings, greetings, greetings!" - Kid coming home in a box (per Country Joe®) and so forth.

Gurgitation

Forced concession can be hard to swallow. Isn't that the truth? As noted on page 16, and again on page 24, Frankie had a problem dealing with it, and he's not alone.

Consider David Dwyer.

Go ahead, I can wait.

Y'know, there are times when you can't help but imagine where you'd be today, if only.

If only you'd thought a little further ahead, for example, when you ignored the warning sign on that trail leading to Radium Hot Springs—the one in Arizona or the one up in British Columbia, take your pick. How long were you in the hospital that time? A couple of weeks, as I remember it. And lucky, really, that you picked B.C. given the excellence of the Canadian healthcare system.

Or when you bought those *chalupas* from a street vendor[80] in *Matamoros?* I mean, couldn't you *tell,* just by *looking,* that it was *incompleto?* Talk about food that ought not have been gurgitated! I don't suppose I need to remind you about the *secuelas!*[81] *Regurgitación* is never pretty.

Oh, sorry, I didn't mean *you:* When I said "you," two paragraphs uphill, I was talking to Don Fulton, Ellen's hubby, while I let you think about Dave Dwyer.

Don certainly had his share of misadventures back before he met Ellen. She's pretty much kept him out of trouble since they itemized. He certainly hasn't driven his car off the road again, like he did that time outside of Prescott, has he? Y'know, up in Chino Valley?

That was a scene, let me tell you! He and his then girlfriend were in his blue '65 Volkswagen Squareback® (what they called a Type III, back in the day). The Type III shared an engine with low-end Porches®, and it was a screamer.

Don was showing off, scaring Ronnie to death; he must have hit ninety on that long, straight stretch.

---

80 *Vendedor ambulante* for you Spanish speakers in the crowd.

81 On a roll with *Español,* are we not?

"You're scaring me," said Ronnie.

He didn't answer.

She said, "What if a dog ran out in front of you?" She paused for dramatic effect, then shouted, "Right NOW!"

Don's hands jerked involuntarily and the car went into a 540° spin, off the pavement into the berm, fortunately hitting nothing substantial, but with the back hatch open and all of their school books, day packs and so forth strewn into the sagebrush.[82]

"Missed the dog," he said chuckling. "And didn't roll!"

"Idiot. We were up on two wheels for a sec."

Climbing out they discovered that three of the four tires had flattened, the beads having popped free of the rims as the auto had careened across the pavement.

Just then a motorcyclist came roaring past and circled back. "Need some help?"

Ronnie spoke up. "I need a ride." With which she hopped on the back of the bike. "See you later Don."[83]

She came back a half-hour or so later, by the way, in the group home van, and Don had the three flats off—one replaced by the spare. He'd collected the items that had erupted from the car.

I could go on.

But now, what do you recall about Mr. Dwyer?

Yes, of course: He was on that jury that convicted Greta Strenberg, and? And?

Don't you read the papers? Or at least your RSS feed? I mean ... Really?

Dwyer is that fellow who founded the Slick Wiccan Chicken® shop on Patton Ave. about eighteen months ago. Does that ring any bells? The only restaurant in America that suggested —though we all knew it was just "in fun"—that ingredients in their chicken pot pies included "Eye of newt, and toe of frog, Wool of bat, and tongue of dog, Adder's fork, and blind-worm's sting, Lizard's leg, and howlet's wing."

I mean, people here in Asheville are sophisticated enough to recognize a little Shakespeare when they see it, having been treated to Shake in the Park all these years—almost 50, wowza!

It seemed like part of the general spirit of keeping Asheville weird. Y'know? A cross-dressing nun on a bicycle, more

82 This actually happened to your humble author, with genders reversed. Susan was kind of crazy at times.

83 This too, but genders not reversed. FYI.

breweries per capita than any city in Germany, black bears wandering around downtown and Slick Wiccan Chicken®.

The food was good, as was business, right up until that biologist at Western Carolina University® ran a DNA test.

That story bifurcated pretty fast, remember?

Not a trace of blind-worm or howlet in the mix. The local coven filed a lawsuit claiming false advertising and launched a boycott.

Meanwhile the health department put the kibosh on the outfit, noting that the USDA didn't even have a grading system for newt, bat, dog or lizard parts. (Frogs legs and snake were deemed OK, and Dave claimed that the "lizard" in the mix was actually alligator, so he got a pass from the health folks there, but that only further infuriated the witches.)

The local Shakespeare troupe, which had been negotiating a joint advertising effort, dropped Slick Wiccan Chicken® like a hot rock, and meanwhile some local Evangelicals were suggesting that burning at the stake was too good for Dave. (The Chamber of Commerce hinted that a ducking stool was a better choice now that the River Arts District greenway was complete. The ducking event itself would draw a crowd, and then the Ducked David Dwyer Memorial could be added as a stop on the Urban Trail.

Surely you didn't miss all *that!*

I really don't know what this world is coming to.

[Sigh.]

BTW, Dave sold the shop and fled for parts unknown, an appropriate destination given that unknown parts figured so prominently in his mix. More about the shop anon.

Deflated

If you're imagining one of those puffed up front yard Santas when the power goes off you're on the right track. Looking a little floppy, particularly when the breeze kicks up, aren't we? A little bereft.

That surely describes Nadine just now.

And wouldn't we all? Be? Deflated?

Nadine, as we were reminded on page 32, is an old-timer in these parts, having first been recruited in the mid to late 90s. I suppose "old timer" makes her sound old, and that's not quite true. Late 40s. But having lived in short story form for close to 25 years is nothing to sneeze at, nor is her handiwork. She was a skilled trim carpenter when we first met and she's continually upped her game.

The banister she created for the sweeping staircase in the Morehead mansion? Absolutely exquisite! Those balusters? That look like tangled vines? Nothing like it anywhere that I've been, and I'd bet five bucks the same is true for you.

Maybe the Moreheads will throw a wingding when the house is finished and you'll get your chance, assuming that it's an "open house" affair. If it's invitation only ... well, lots of luck there. I don't even think *I'd* be invited, and I helped install the damn railing. It was much too heavy for Nadine to install alone and she knew I had the time, so she gave me a call. [Sorry for the burst of ill temper. But I'm feeling a little peeved at the moment.]

I should add here that while she built the curved staircase —a production that is a rare bit of handiwork in this era of cold efficiency and late-stage capitalism—and designed the balusters and created the banister itself (from multiple pieces of ash, joined so expertly that it is hard to find the seams), she did not carve the vines.

Credit where due: Nutter Knudsen, the wood carver we met in the very first story in *Waist Not, Want Knot,*[84] was pleased to accept the commission and did an outstanding job. Oh, and by the way, he and Lurlene are doing just fine, thank you. Seems like that tetradrachm was lucky after all. Life with a nudist is thrilling.

---

84 Brave Ulysses Books, 2020

You're doubtless wondering one of two things at this point.

1. How did Nadine happen to know Nutter?
Perhaps collaterally:
1.a) Did she read about him in *Waist Not?*
Or:
2. Is the Martin mentioned as Nadine's boyfriend on page 32 (in reference to her first appearance in fictive form in or about 1997) actually Nutter's brother, who supposedly first emerged in 2020?
And collaterally:
2.a) If so, did that relationship occur before or after he married Barbara? [We thought they married out of college.]

You *have* been paying attention after all! I am so proud of you! I had to go back myself to see, and gosh, I *wrote* that story!

What I've determined is that I didn't leave any time slot on Martin Knudsen's dance card where he might have had a couple of years to live with Nadine when she was in her 20s. So, nope. Not the same Martin, which is kind of a shame when I stop to think about it.

As perspicacious as you seem to be, I'm certain you can see the problem here. I invented *two different* Martins when one would have done just fine, expending my creativity when it was completely unnecessary. [Like phlogiston, we only get so much, and then we run out :-(←this is a frowny face.] If I'd suggested, say, that Martin and Barb had met some years *after* college, there would have been time enough for Nadine and Martin to shack up.

To be perfectly honest, something for which I'm known, if Nade[85] had, in fact, met the Knudsen Martin they might still be together. That Marty,[86] we recall, was quite the intellectual and would hardly have scoffed at her philosophic insights. Whereas the former cohabitee Martin wasn't exactly "deep." Our carpentress was and is, and she left him far behind.

C'est la vie. As is said in Francophone realms.

But that didn't particularly deflate her: *Comme ci comme ça*[87] is her view of relationships. Some good, some not so much, and "This too shall pass" covers a whole lot of ground. Anyway, she's between men right now and not really looking around.

---

85 Righto! A hypocoristic!

86 Ditto.

87 *Così così* in Italian.

As to question number one—in fact, yes. Nadine, as has been indicated, is intellectually curious and consequently ordered a copy of *Waist Not* as soon as it hit the shelves. Then, needing an expert woodcarver for her project, she e-mailed me to get contact info for Nutter. [cecilbothwell@gmail.com]

You see, there is a practical side to reading top-notch short fiction, and I'd be more than happy to connect you to any of the characters herein if you have need. You good eggs at least.

But, hey, I just got an e-mail from Henry in Black Mountain [Wow! That was quick!] who wants to know who these Moreheads are, how they made so much money, and where in heck is the much-storied mansion? We'll have to get back to Nadine in a bit.

Francis Morehead is the owner of a cloth patch stitching company. That may seem like an unimportant niche market sort of item, but you'd be surprised! There are all sorts of places—mostly uniforms, natch—that sport embroidered patches. The organization formerly known as Boy Scouts®, for one, and police and fire people, and EMTs and bowling leagues and Girl Scouts® and Army, Air Force, Navy, Marines, Coast Guard, and the much hyped new United States Space Force. College teams and pro ball, too.

Wait. I thought there were eight uniformed services in the You Ess of Ay? Oh, right, the United States Public Health Service Commissioned Corps. [How easily we forget. Maybe one of my characters can work for them. Hmmm.]

And, umm. It's right on the tip of my tongue. Ummm. Ah. Oh. The National Oceanic and Atmospheric Administration Commissioned Officer Corps.

It's kind of encouraging to know that there are uniformed people taking care of the water and air. I think. I truly mean "kind of"—honestly, they could do better, what with Flint and the 400 ppb of carbon in the atmosphere. You know?

Anyway, Francis is third generation in the biz and has long-term contracts with some of the patchiest, so he's set. [Kind of astonishing that there are actually *three* patch embroidery operations in the greater Asheville area, don'cha think?]

The mansion is being built on Beaucatcher Mountain, overlooking Asheville with a sweeping view of mountains to the south and west. Worth noting here that while it qualifies as a manse due to the extraordinary quality of the workmanship, it isn't really huge. Only about 4,500 square feet. Nothing like the stonepiles some of the *nouveau riche* assemble.

[Mr. Gore? Mr. Bush? Here's looking at you, kids. 10,000 and 8,000 respectively? Really? Bill Gates? 66 fricking thousand? What?]

That bit out of the way, back to Nadine. We were considering the idea that she seemed bereft for some unspecified reason. I'll have to come up with something.

While I'm mulling I can tell you that the look on her face is semi-tragic. As indicated upslope, kind of how you look when you see a saggy Santa, but not, say, how you'd look if a Mall Santa died while your four-year-old was sitting on his lap.

Remember Mall Santas? Back before the time of cholera? Those were the days, my friend.

Nadine's brow is furrowed, her lips are puckered, her eyes are downcast and she's stroking her chin. But no tears that could make this scene trend more to the tragic.

Oh, I've got it.

I just remembered she uses a Paslode® gas-activated angle finish nailer these days. You likely recall that back when we first met her she was wrapping a room with molding and being very careful not to kiss the wood with her hammer. For those of you who don't have a copy of *Archaic* handy, I quote:

> Careful avoidance of kissing is the mark of the master carpenter. Nadine was consummately careful as she wrapped the room with wainscoting and crown, base and shoe. "Kissing," The Observer[88] thought of Martin, and, latterly of Bob, "is plumbing."
> She wondered if Bob was still in residential wiring. They had broken up—was it three years already?[89] "Electricity." The whisper attached itself to an involuntary lick of the upper lip. "E-lectricity," she breathed it slowly, "is kissing." Careful not to kiss she tapped another nail home, centered the punch and tapped again. "Action central."

Using a nail gun obviates the threat of hammer dents ("kisses" in the carpenterial argot) and does a really nice job of countersinking the nails if the pressure adjustment is correct.

---

88 Nadine was cast as "The Observer" in that story.

89 This reminds me that I didn't leave time in Nadine's life for a romance with the Knudsen Martin either. So it wouldn't have mattered if I'd delayed the marriage to Barbara. Good to have that settled.

It also, obviously, eliminates the use of a punch.

Some carpenters prefer air actuated nail guns because over time they're cheaper to operate, but Nadine and I agree that the extra cost is really negligible and the noise of a compressor is bothersome, while the hoses are a pain in the neck and a tripping hazard besides. Nowadays you can get rechargeable ones that don't even use fuel, but once you've paid $400 for a tool you aren't generally in a hot hurry to replace it.

However, everything put together falls apart sooner or later. Even, say, an anvil, which looks about as unlikely to fall apart as anything put together can look. (A shot put perhaps somewhat more so. Or do I mean less so?)

But, as Neil Young once reminded us, "Rust never sleeps."

[Now I've done it. I'm going to lose sleep wondering how long it takes for a shot put to rust away to nothing.]

In this instance the nail gun quit firing.

The way it's supposed to work goes like this: It won't fire just by pulling the trigger. You have to press down hard, which forces a slide up into the body of the tool, releasing the safety lock and also sending a quick squirt of propellant gas into the firing cylinder and turning on an internal fan which evenly disperses the fuel. Pulling the trigger sends a jolt of electricity to the spark plug and the gas explodes, driving the piston down so the driver head forces the fastener into whatever you happen to be nailing.

So, obviously, there are multiple points at which the system might fail. She checked the fuel. Plenty. She took the top off and examined the spark plug. A little carbony, but seemed OK. The slide was mechanically intact and the trigger mechanism tested OK with her voltmeter. [She'd learned a little about electricity from Bob, between kisses and before ... but no, I don't want to digress. Go back to *Archaic* if you want the story of the difficulty she encountered with Bob. The jerk.]

[Not a good egg FWIW.]

She DuckDucked® and found her answer—which she might have done first and saved a bit of time. The blinking light was alternating red and green, which indicated a system failure most often caused by a defective fan motor. She ordered one three weeks ago and it arrived last Thursday.

In the meantime she had attempted to remove the fan blades from the old motor (sold separately) and found that to be impossible, so she ordered a new fan, which arrived today.

Finally! [She'd become way tired of having dozens of parts

spread out on the kitchen counter, and getting shut of the clutter was almost as appealing as having the tool in working condition.]

Everything went back together just fine right up until the final assembly of the spring-loaded track that held nails and fed them to the power head. The main spring was no problem. But there was a tiny spring, about as long as a smallish vitamin capsule, and she was baffled about where it belonged.

Such bafflement could be the proximate cause of her knitted brow, but no. She looked at the schematic in the user's manual, which showed the spring with a thin line indicating where it should go, but the line disappeared behind another part in the drawing, making the damned thing's proper placement utterly unclear. So near and yet ...

She was turning it over and over, trying to make some sense of it, when her phone rang. It was Dominic Hazelton, whom you'll recall she met on that jury, offering to take her to dinner.

As noted, she hasn't been shopping around, but she isn't averse to a date, particularly now, what with the quarantine and all, and he was suggesting take-out and dining socially distanced in the park down by the river. She's been careful and he assured her that he has as well, and has, in fact, tested negative within the last few days. So she's good to go.

After she hung up she went back to her task.

But now the spring is/was missing.

She's been standing there, not two feet from the counter, for about ten minutes. Neither Big Mama nor Fulton[90] has jumped up there. Where in hell can that spring have run off to?

Where indeed?

Wind out of her sails for certain.

Hope may spring eternal, but absent the spring, what then? Does hope simply fall? Is nothing eternal?

<):-(} ←Sad Santa.

Sad Nadine →)-:b ←Ball cap

Sad excuse for a story? I'll try harder next time.

---

90 If it's not clear: her cats.

Giving Up

That last gave me a great idea! It's really exciting when a slight digression blooms so perfectly—not unlike, I think it's safe to say, forcing paperwhites in the wintertime when nothing outside is in bloom. Just add water!

Having said that, I suppose I'd be doing some of my readers a favor if I added step-by-step instructions. It will save you DuckDuckGoing and such.

1. Purchase three paperwhite bulbs at a hardware or nursery in the fall.
2. Procure an eight-inch container with no hole in the bottom. (That is to say, not a "regular" flower pot.)
3. Procure enough pebbles to fill said container.
4. Fill the container halfway with pebbles.
5. Place the three bulbs in the pot, rootlets down.
6. Add the rest of the pebbles, and add enough water that it reaches the rootlets of the bulbs.
7. Place the pot in a closet or other dark space for a week or so. (Or not, if you prefer shorter flowers.)
8. Place the pot in a sunny location.

Enjoy!

It really bolsters this writer's confidence to know that, whatever the inestimable value of all else he has composed, there are, sprinkled here and there, solid tips about this sort of thing. Or, say, the correct temperature for curing concrete on page 49. Or helping to steer my readers around the temptation to participate in a demolition derby (page 43) or, for that matter, ignoring the warning signs at Radium Hot Springs (page 53—and that applies to either the British Columbia or Arizona outpost). Or the warning regarding experimental aircraft that will help you to "Live long and prosper" [91] which you'll happily discover on page 90.

I feel like I'm making a small difference.

---

91 In Mr. Spock's Star Trekkian® Vulcan sign language.

Sadly, Dominic Hazelton thought he was making a "small difference" too, but no. It turned fruitless.[92] He hoped, and still entertains hopes as far as I know, nor has he lost some semblance of an eternal spring, but—and it's a big but—in this era of late-stage capitalism his work was doomed by politics.

"What does Dominic do?" You ask.

Captain Hazelton works in the National Oceanic and Atmospheric Administration Commissioned Officer Corps. (See? I knew this "service division" trivia thing would come in handy!)

As we well recall, NOAA COMCOR® conducts surveys and studies and analysis, and the officers get to wear uniforms with patches! Having worn a uniform myself, in high and far off times, I can attest to how good that can feel, assuming you're proud of the particular organization involved.

As a former Eagle Scout I can attest that I had a whole lot of embroidered patches: rank insignia, merit badges, summer camp logos, trail mementos, camporees, jamborees and even Philmont Scout Ranch®. I had a synthetic chamois cloth vest festooned with the things. [In my own "small way" contributing to the construction of the Morehead mansion mentioned on page 56.]

I think it was my great good fortune to have had inspiring leaders, fine peers and generally uplifting experiences, as well as to have sold all my memorabilia on eBay® before the Boy Scouts of America® crashed and burned amid charges of sexual misconduct. I'd imagine prices on collectibles have fallen.

Lest I be seen as unsentimental or debasing in my mercantile attitude toward badges of honor, I'd point out that the relict BSA® is now selling its Norman Rockwell® collection to help settle 82,000 sex abuse claims (and art experts are stepping forward to say that they are kind of schmaltzy and not really Rockwell's® best work.) So I'm not the only former Scout who's cashed in.

Capt. Hazelton's area of expertise involves managing land surveys. It's important work, nor is it limited to the simple task of determining whether land is still where it used to be, which I think, absent devastating earthquakes or nuclear bombardment, more or less goes without saying.

---

92 Reminding us of Bernard Milton, Ph.D., the former ag researcher in the stirring parable about the Green Revolution, population growth and the U.S. Postal Service® in "Wisdom Tooth," *Self-Evident,* BUB, 2021.

He actually started out in the private sector and was one of those people you see around your neighborhood from time to time operating a laser transit, nailing blue ribbons into the asphalt or tying orange ribbons to branches and tree trunks, either divvying things up or sorting things out—things like whose fence is encroaching on whom, or who owns the tree that just fell on a Subaru®. It's all a lot more scientific and disputative these days than "from the old elm stump by the creek to the big rock" and that sort of thing. Eventually, however, Dominic wanted to fry bigger fish.

And fish, we will see, are what lead us to the nubbin of this story.

Fish, as we all (or most of us, anyway) know, live in water.

They also, as at least some of us know, breed in water.

Many, as a few among us know, breed in estuaries.

There's the rub.

Dominic (which he prefers to the formality of rank) has overseen coastal surveys from Virginia south to Florida for the past several years and has carefully documented sea level rise, relying on both current and historical data. You can see the problem, I'm sure.

Sometimes he can't sleep at night. My guess is that if you were as familiar with the facts of the matter as he, you would have the same problem, so I'll not go into it here. Alarmed would not be the half of it.

A few nights after his dinner date with Nadine (see page 61)—which, by the way, they both thoroughly enjoyed, it being a lovely spring evening and each finding the other's company most pleasant—he found his thoughts so fraught that he texted her at three a.m., not intending to wake her and assuming her ringer was off, as is his when he's attempting to sleep, only to be surprised at her quick response.

- didn't mean to wake you
- didn't – you OK?
- subsidence or rise – plagues me
- FWIW IMHO – rise
- UR right, but hope springs for former
- get that would b BTR
- rise scares me – 2 death
- get that – doomed we R – S2aries gone!
- doomed indeed!!!

You can see right there how aligned these two fine folks are, and why they might very easily fall in love. People like your author who are routinely awake at three a.m. are in a class of their own, to coin a phrase. We fret about the state of the planet and drink coffee in the wee hours, rising early in order to get the essential worrying done before the day-to-day draws our attention to the things that *must* be done to ensure mere short-term survival.

It's a matter of experience, really. You simply aren't going to agonize over the fate of the world while you're measuring detergent for a load of laundry, or vacuuming the living room, or sweeping the front walk, or weeding—oh, boy, especially not when you're weeding—or trimming a hedge, or eating a hard-boiled egg, or brushing your teeth for that matter, or going from stand to stand at the farmers' market, or driving to work if you're not working from home, or roping steers, or pleading a case, or feeding your tropical fish, or wiping your windshield while filling 'er up with powerful gasoline, or operating a cash register, or drawing blood from a patient, or teaching, or trying to teach the unteachable, or filing either paperwork or nails.

Which reminds me of a very funny thing that happened to a local nonprofit organization here in Asheville.

The nonprofit, which shall here remain nameless, was an organization that did,—or purported to do—good. It was aimed at alleviating discrimination in the public sphere, but if I offer more details on that score I would be giving too much away, and in any event that isn't directly involved in what makes this so funny.

The nonprofit ran into financial trouble when the IRS came down on them like John Henry or Thor, hammer and tongs, revoking their nonprofit status and imposing steep fines. This organization had been funded by the federal government via a pass-through by the local government, which municipality immediately canceled the relevant contract.

Quel désastre![93]

Here comes the funny part. Are you ready?

Part of the office manager's remit was to file tax returns every year—returns that had been duly prepared by the office bookkeeper.

Sure enough, she had filed them!

For years!

---

93 We haven't used a French phrase for a while and I thought this would help emphasize the scope of the problem.

In a file drawer!

In a file drawer![94]

I so hope you weren't drinking coffee just now.

Where was I? Oh, early morning worrying. Right. So, you see, we who devote ourselves to pondering the imponderable, to questioning the unquestionable, to assessing the unassessable, start bright and early every day, to get that out of the way.

It's OK if you're not one of us and just sleep in. We won't talk about you behind your back or anything, or look down our noses. We can handle it, just fine on our own, thanks. We're sort of like the bakers and the newspaper deliverers and the burglars[95] and buglers who rise and shine before everyone else in order to get the world going each morning.

Which, as such things will, reminds me of one of my father's favorite songs.

"Someday I'm going to murder the bugler, someday they're going to find him dead. And then I'll get the other pup, the one who gets the bugler up, and spend all the rest of my life in bed."

"But what?" you ask. "What does any of that have to do with the title of this story?"

I thought that was plain enough, but for those of you who can't take a hint ... [Sigh.] ... Dominic has decided to quit NOAA COMCOR® and take a job with the U.S. Postal Service®. He's given up on trying to persuade the North Carolina General Assembly® to accept facts as a basis for policy.

The Republican majority in the good old Tarheel State has decreed that climate change is a myth and that the sea level will not rise more than eight inches. Ever. Therefore no state publication can indicate otherwise, making Dominic's work on the state's coast, for NOAA COMCOR®, fruitless. He's tired of banging his head against that wall. He's fried bigger fish and failed, so like many of my better protagonists he has headed for the USPS®, where the work actually benefits the recipients of his endeavors.

94 This is absolutely a true story. You really can't make stuff like this up.

95 More about burglary anon.

Knot of Toads

Isn't that an interesting phrase? I so wish I'd known about this when I composed the stories in *Waist Not, Want Knot,* since it would clearly have fit in so well and seems so obviously out of place here. But we have to gather rosebuds when and while we may, and this one came my way during my morning consult[96] with a *NYT*® crossword the day before yesterday. Right up until 3:41 a.m. on Monday, January 25, 2021, whilst solving a puzzle dated Friday, February 27, 2015, I had no idea that a gathering of the dry-skinned members of the family *Bufonidae*[97] is properly referred to as a “knot.”

This is something I really ought to have known fifty-four years ago when I was a Boy Scout® merit badge counselor at a summer camp, teaching, among other things, Reptile Study.[98] How many lives would have been changed had I known? It's one thing for me to realize today how much poorer my life has been due to that inexcusable lapse in my education, but now my conscience is weighted down with the fate of all of my students. The poor lads!

In the same clue I was reminded that a cluster of owls is a parliament. This I did know then, so my Bird Study merit badge students were not short-sheeted like the others, or like our camp director's bed. [Oh, the pranks we pulled!]

This came up again in this morning's puzzle (Friday, February 20, 2015): “Participants in Britain's question time, briefly.” The answer being, obviously enough, “MPs.”

But here's the thing, or one thing, that tells me my time spent at crucigrams is not wasted. Through all the years I've known that the barred, screech, barn, saw whet, burrowing, snowy and other owls I've heard and seen all across this vast

---

96 Unlike the activities described on page 65, solving a crossword puzzle in no way interferes with fretting about our common future. FYI.

97 Latin! Isn't Latin fun?

98 It was “Reptile Study” back then, and as my good friend Zefan pointed out, that should not have included amphibians. So I looked it up and he was correct: The badge has been renamed “Reptile and Amphibian Study.” Atta boy Zefan!

continent, in woods and fields, in tundra and desert, met as a parliament, it never before this morning struck me that the reason for the appellation stems from Britain's "question time" with its shouting MPs.

"Who? Who?"

This makes so much sense now! I yield the floor.

Knot of Toads
Photo credit: Lang Elliot

musicofnature.com

(I apologize if this seems a little too graphic for young'uns.)

Sweet Surrender

"It doesn't mean much
It doesn't mean anything at all
The life I've left behind me
Is a cold room"

Sarah McLachlan there, and can we argue? No, we can't. First of all because, in fairness, she isn't here just now for purposes of debate, and, secondly, the experienced temperature of a room is highly variable depending on a wide range of factors. Maybe she forgot her sweater when she went into a recording studio—did you ever think of that? Maybe she has iron-poor-tired-blood and needs a shot of Geritol®? Maybe she grew up in a walk-in freezer? An igloo? [After all, she is Canadian and you "know" those Canucks.]

I mean to say, I really adore her songs—and what's not to love about her voice? But in my line of work we constantly face the need to discover meaning, and while the chorus ...

"Swee-eet surrender"[99]

... seems absolutely on target for a collection with the current title, the verses are puzzling. So I went and watched the "official video." Things only got worse.

She's driving a car and runs "herself" over[100] and the body ends up on the back seat, and then she's dragging her body out of the car, up a path, and then carrying her corpse into a building. Next she's lying on a futon and her dead—or rather "dying,"—body is under that sofa, twitching. Then she kind of morphs from dead or dying to alive, back and forth, with lots of close-ups of her face, singing, naturally, and so on and so forth. All kind of dreamy. She is quite pretty, of course, which counts for something.

99 "Sweet Surrender" from the album *Surfacing,* Arista Records,1997

100 Reminding me of Aunt Toop (hypocoristic of Tupelo) whom we got to know in "Sally's Fourth," in the astonishing collection *Can We Have Archaic and Idiot? 2,* Brave Ulysses Books, 2009/2018

The music is exquisite, but the story line?

Not exactly what we in the trade call "linear." (Unlike all of my output, I would here note. I am reliable: "Second to the right, and straight on till morning," as the saying goes.)

We're going to have to look elsewhere for a "sweet surrender" that makes more sense, or so it seems to me. And given that we have a jury pool to pull from, let's go with William Bryce.

Bill is just an average Joe, really, when you get right down to it. His was one of the "open minds" during Greta Strenberg's trial for alleged theft of a *Noblet*®[101] clarinet, and even if he landed on the wrong end of the facts of the matter, it was an honest choice. It's not like he was alone in that travesty of justice.

More accurate, perhaps, to say Bill is just an "average particle physicist." A cosmologist. Could be you or me, really. And like us he's way deep into the Standard Model®. Way, way deep.

Aren't we all? Aren't we all?

[Using a judicious "we" here. Because some are not, and we know about *those people*. But *we* are better than that. Right?]

That's how you can tell he's "average."

If he weren't, well, I guess it goes without saying that he'd be a "Standard Model Skeptic.®" Some of *those people* don't even put their pants on one leg at a time, if you get my drift. Once a person wanders off into the dark side of dark matter and neutrino mass ... um, axions anyone? Let's just say you wouldn't want to invite them into your home. There are limits, and we can't be too careful.

The other thing about Bill is that he bathes regularly. This might seem like kind of a small thing, assuming you don't have to work beside him for long stretches (though, of course, no one is working beside anyone for long stretches in this time of cholera.) But the point is that some particle physicists get so obsessed with things that *no one can even see*—and that may or not even *exist*—that they forget about personal hygiene. Kind of a forest/trees thing, only on a submicroscopic scale. But not our Bill.

On the other hand I wouldn't want you to think he's an obsessive clean-freak. Just normal showering and shaving and clipping of nails and so forth. Changes his underwear regularly as well. For which I'm quite certain his wif,e Janet, is grateful. Having a spouse whose million- mile gaze at breakfast is closer to

101 Got to say *"Noblet®"* again. Coolbeanz or what? Page 34 if memory has failed you. Y'know, the trial scene?

million-light-year glare is tolerable, but if he smelled funny? Not so much.

Now that we've met Janet we can move along to the story part of the story, for which I can see you've been eager.

Janet is a tolerant soul. When Bill's thoughts stray off to some distant black hole, parsing the shredding of time and matter at some sort of event horizon, she's perfectly content to busy herself with kitchen appliances like the Klein bottle she keeps in a cabinet to the left of the over-the-stove microwave. She knows that having a non-orientable surface with no boundary can be the key to a happy marriage. When his attention is riveted by some impossibly distant *malstrøm,*[102] her focus is slipping and sliding along a two-dimensional manifold against which a system for determining a normal vector cannot be consistently defined.

Meaning, I'm sure you understand, that she daydreams.

However, we must here observe that she is not what the Monkees® referred to as a "Daydream Believer." She's a daydream "visitor," surfing her inconsistently defined vector when it pleases her and then back to the "real world." Sort of a non-orientable surface "long-boarder." ("We ride the waves, distance is gone, will we find out, how life began?"[103])

Back on planet Earth she is a lifeguard at a YWCA® pool. Preventing the drowning of youngsters is about as far from surfing non-normal vectors as it gets, and she's a pro. Janet knows the ropes regarding water safety and has never lost a swimmer yet!

Oh, there was that one time—that *one* time—that things almost got out of hand, or, rather, remained submerged overlong, but she saved the day! I'm sure you read about it. Getting to the bottom of things and not resurfacing is not a good "outcome" in a twelve-foot-deep *svømmepøl.*[104] But, and here's the important fact, the brain damage could have been worse. Jimmy can still nod his head.

The more interesting thing here, I think, is how it happens that she has a Klein bottle in the kitchen cabinet. Am I right?

The Klein bottle was a gift from Bill. This is the kind of imaginary object that a particle physicist is inclined [in-Kleined?], perhaps driven by the solar wind, to give a loved one.

Just think of it. On Christmas morning Janet pulls the

102 Danish! We didn't expect Danish did we?

103 Stray lyric from the Moody Blues®.

104 And again! Janet *née* Pedersdatter would appreciate this.

gaily decorated package from beneath the tree. Bill smiles, perhaps gives her a quick peck on the cheek, and says, “I hope you like it.”

Unwrapped and then unboxed, there–it wasn't. Janet exclaimed, “Oh, honey! It's like nothing I've ever seen! I never imagined! It's beyond my wildest dreams!”

Bill quipped, “It's homeomorphic to the connective sum of two projective planes.”

“I *get* that. How did you know I wanted one?”

“Honey, I treasure your singularity.”

OK, I hear you thinking, so Bill couldn't come up with a gift idea, he wraps an empty box and then convinces Janet that there's “something” there–a concept really. A thing that only exists in our minds because it can't be constructed in three-dimensional space.

Isn't that kind of a lame gift? Wouldn't an obsidian knife have been more tangible? And practical, as well, in terms of getting to the hearts of matters?[105] [And those of *forælders* and *datters* and *søns?*]

To which I'd reply, “Lame is in the eye of the beholder, unless we're talking about an actual leg problem.”

You ask, “Does Janet have an actual leg problem?”

“It depends on what you'd consider a problem.”

“What do you mean?”

“Well, ever since she received that *lovely thoughtful and heartfelt gift* from her hubby she's been working at putting her pants on both legs at a time. I think he inspired her.”

“How's that going?”

“About how you'd expect. It didn't work with bluejeans so she moved along to sweatpants. That wasn't much better. Even with the fire pole she installed so she could land on both feet at once.”

“So did she give up?”

“Yep. Sweat surrender I guess.”

“It doesn't mean much
It doesn't mean anything at all
The life I've left behind me
Is a cold room”

(At least, in her sweats, she isn't cold. There's that.)

105 See Aztec references, pages 13 and 22. I just knew this was going to be a “thing” here.

Getting Low

Honesty is reputedly the best policy, though most of us lie a lot of the time, which suggests that we don't really believe it. Likely better to say that it reflects well on a person to stake that claim.

But here, right here, I'm going to be completely honest with you. I came "this close" to titling the present little gem "Letting Go" before I abruptly realized I'd used that way back on page 20. My sense is that I do plenty to confuse my readers without including two stories in a collection with the same title. I can just hear the Book Club discussions now,[106] and so I've wisely chosen a different route.

"Getting Low" suggested itself immediately, given its easy alliteration from the other, although tying it to a cede may be a little more complicated. But I'm feeling up to it at the moment.

You with strong memories will immediately realize that Ned Fowler was *not* on the jury that convicted Greta Strenberg, so you're probably wondering where on earth I dug him up.

Well, let's see, how about this: he was in the jury *pool* but was rejected when the prosecuting attorney learned that his hobby was collecting pre-Columbian obsidian knives.[107] The D.A. believed, and he's probably correct, that while a surveyor like Dominic Hazelton would be susceptible to "facts on the ground," an archeological anthropologist was more likely to imagine that "facts on the ground" could be interpreted in several different ways, leading to a sense of uncertainty about guilt or innocence.

I mean, think for a moment of Charles Mann.

See what I mean?

So Ned wasn't tapped for jury duty. He wasn't even tapped as an alternate in case one of the other jurors flaked out during the grueling nearly two hour long trial, which meant he

106 "Are you on page 21 or page 75? Are you talking about that woman dentist with the missing Miata® or some other woman Bothwell invents two pages from here?"

107 It isn't clear to me why these keep popping up—or sinking in, as the case so often may be.

was free to go on his peripatetic way—which further meant that the events you are about to encounter were thus enabled.

I don't think it's a bridge too far to lay what ensued at the feet of D.A. Dan Appler. Sure, we know he's a good egg as D.A.s go, but his dismissal of Ned ... well, well.

To make a short story long we'll follow Ned out the door of the fourth floor courtroom and down the stairs, a narrow set of steps accessed between the elevator shafts, down two floors and then descending a broad marble staircase that winds around in the front section of the building and down to the main floor.

The merest cursory examination of marble treads will explain to even the dimmest of wits why it is that statuary has been carved from the material for thousands of years. Simple shoes have worn the distal noses of those things, smoothing and smoothing them in just one century's use, making it easy to imagine how chisel and mallet might shape the substrate in the hands of a dedicated artist. Ned thought of this as he trod.

Thence Ned descended the short flight of connecting steps to the exit doors, which back in the good old days permitted both ingress and egress. Alas, the realities of modern gun culture now require that all entrants to the building come in by way of a single door on a lower level, thence to run all one's possessions through an x-ray scanner and one's person through a metal detector, only to be wanded by an unsmiling deputy if one's belt buckle or prosthetic limb sets off an alarm.

[Note here: Ned's artificial extremity was necessitated by an accident at a dig in central Mexico. If I were to squander precious pixels here relating that catastrophe, you'd surely agree that he was lucky to survive. You'll just have to trust me on this as I have othere weighty matters on my mind at present. It is, by the way, a high-quality prosthesis, and he barely limps.[108]]

Now down a few more steps to the plaza, then a right turn, and across the principal downtown east-west boulevard, hurrying through the freezing rain to the parking deck. There he rides an elevator to the fifth level where he left his car a couple of hours earlier.

I'm hearing some grumbling. So you're saying you *don't want* the whole story? The slow drive down the ramped parking deck, spiraling, spiraling to the catacombs where the exit station sits, there to pay for three hours parked since he's a few minutes

108 Unlike Janet, in the previous story, I'm sorry to have had to say that Ned *does* have a leg problem. But he's coping well.

past two? Or the friend who waved from under a large blue umbrella as he approached the street ...

OK, OK. Have it your way. I'll just cut to the chase, though there wasn't actually a "chase" involved. That's just a manner of speaking or, more accurately, a "figure of speech."

Ned lives a ways out of town. A thirty-five-minute drive when there's no traffic, but it was just past noon and lunchtime traffic was thick and further slowed by the foul weather. Unlucky there, I think we'd agree, since he was quite anxious to get back to work.

"What work?" is doubtless the first question that comes to your mind, and I'm prepared to come up with something right this minute.

We already know that he's an archeological anthropologist, which is a solid hint. And we recall the invitation for readers to consider Charles Mann, which is another. In addition we learned that the dreadful accident that nearly took Ned's life occurred in the course of a "dig" south of the border. So I think we can infer that the lodestone drawing him home in a hot hurry had somewhat to do with Mesoamerican culture, and we're right!

There was an online "webinar" scheduled for the selfsame morning [with a break for lunch] as the soon-to-become-infamous clarinet trial, and, had Ned been tapped for the jury, he would have missed it entirely. As it was he'd be able to at least catch the second session. This one involved his area of particular expertise, the Olmecs®, and he would definitely be able to inject some important perspectives into the proceedings.

The Olmecs®, we recall, had a dominant land-owning class that significantly shaped their culture at a time when most of the surrounding people were still subsisting at a neolithic level. I mean, the others didn't even have obsidian knives[109] for goodness sake, which just goes to show. Like most land-owning classes they tended to be "big-headed," though in this case and in those high and far-off days, the inclination of the "big-headed" to mask their high falutin'ness with a modicum of tasteful professed humility was not well developed.

Their sculptures of themselves were nine-foot tall heads for gosh sake! Big-headedness writ large.

I'll grant you, the Olmecs® are the earliest known

109 Yes, the Olmecs had—which factoid I didn't know until a few minutes ago when I learned that Ned was an expert in same and looked it up on the Web—obsidian knives! Definitely going to be a "thing!"

civilization in the Americas to have used mathematics and even had the concept of zero,[110] for which they should indeed be accorded some right to pridefulness.

I know you're eager to hear the rest of Ned's difficult day, but this zero thing reminds me of another pre-Columbian culture and how it was disparaged by Europeans. So, a brief digression.

When European Catholic® explorers arrived in Polynesia they were appalled at the backwardness and non-Christianity displayed throughout the islands. So they did the usual murder and so forth to establish that they were God-fearing and holy. Then they confiscated all the cultural artifacts they could find to take home as keepsakes, or burn, as was their wont.

Arriving back in Spain or Portugal or Italy—or wherever—they had a good laugh about the stupid natives. Why, they only had two numbers! Can you imagine?

Buckminster Fuller informed me about the following, and I have to give him full(er) credit, though I don't know for certain that he was the discoverer of this laugh-fest, or even the first to glean this particular bit of insight regarding island math.

Polynesians were able to navigate from island to island across thousands of miles of open ocean thanks to a clever combination of reading the currents, and celestial orientation and math. They had only two numbers, it's true. Like the computer I'm typing on or the cell phone in your pocket. Ones and zeroes work pretty well, IMHO. Binary mathematics is kind of "a thing" nowadays.

But back to Ned. So he's headed home from that courtroom and thinking about the upcoming opportunity to add to an important scholarly discussion and he completely ignores the fact that he's *getting low* on gas.

And he runs out and sputters to a stop on the berm.

"I give up," he says to no one in particular.[111] "I give up."

---

110 Ditto per just now learning this. Hurray for the internet!

111 Which reminds me that I was supposed to invent another character on page 75. It completely slipped my mind. If I'd just had him pick up a hitchhiker! But no hitchhikers were out and about. If it'd been warm and sunny I'm pretty certain Leonora Jensen would have been thumbing a ride home then, given that she'd left her car at the garage with no loaner available. She's an empath and would have been just the person to offer her solicitude to Ned. Then again, if he'd been chatting with Leonora instead of zoning out, lost in thought about Olmecs® he might have noticed his gas gauge, rendering the preceding entirely moot.

Relinquishing

Or *relinquisshen* for you Middle English speakers out there. (You know who you are, you who *refused* to learn to speak French after the Norman conquest. As do we. Know, that is.)

Educated sorts were much more likely to say *abandonner* of course, so you with the *relinquisshen* were doing exactly that—giving away any hope of upward mobility in a very class-conscious society. You're lucky you weren't tossed in the drowning well.

Leonora Jensen, whom we got to know pretty intimately on the previous page, is not one of those. No indeed. When she relinquished her car at Mike's Mechanical® she said not a word in Middle English, and due to the weather, she *Überfordert.*[112]

Leonora is a case in point. At least that's the way I'm inclined to view her. A case in point.

When I learned that she has developed a thriving business growing mushrooms in coffee grounds, well, that told me all I needed to know. She started with one five-gallon bucket, as most of us do, but was she content? No, no, no, she was not.

Eating homegrown shrooms is all well and good. Very good, actually, sautéed in butter. Yum!

Anyway, now she has about fifty buckets under cultivation in her basement and she's selling shiitakes and oysters at the local tailgate market. She collects coffee grounds from local bistros, of course. (Nobody drinks that much coffee on their own or even between the two of them.)

Which brings us to Mel, her significant other.

How "significant" is something you'll have to ask them. Not *insignificant,* that's pretty clear, else they wouldn't be likely to cohabit—though a roommate could probably be significant if said roomie was prompt with rent, did the dishes more than seldom, vacuumed and so on and so forth. Heck, that's better than some marital partners, near as I can tell.

Mel is going to be the protagonist of this parable, so I think we need to get to know him a little better.

Average build, maybe five-ten, brown hair, brown eyes, wears glasses, not hirsute, no beer belly, and like Bill Bryce,

112 German!

whom we grew to know and love on page 70, he bathes regularly. It might go without saying at this point, really, that pretty much all of my "good eggs" bathe regularly, but ... there are exceptions that prove any rule. Or disprove, depending on how we frame it, so I thought it worth mentioning here.

Also, duly noted, in this time of cholera there are probably more who don't, but once did, since they're spending their days in pajamas.

With that out of the way, let's get down to brass tacks.

Mel manages a fried chicken restaurant, a franchise which shall here remain nameless as the author fears legal action like some folks fear mice. Or snakes. [Your humble scribe fears neither of those, FWIW. Lawsuits, on the other hand ... well, best steer a wide circle around incitements to sue. Even if you win, you generally lose—at least time, if not—though rarely not—money.]

Mel's the kind of boss every fast-food worker would love to work for, assuming any American fast-food worker loves to work for the kind of crazy-low wages our current system permits.

Wage rates are above Mel's pay grade, of course. But really. I mean, really? Fast-food slaves in the You Ess of Aye are pegged at $7.25 as we speak, at, say, a McDonalds®. And just yesterday—Thursday, February 4, 2021—the U.S. Senate voted once again not to raise the minimum wage. [This makes me want to use strong language, but I am demonstrating restraint.] Workers at McDonalds'® in northern Europe are making $22 per hour, and the franchises there are still turning a profit. Let's repeat that, *"Still turnng a profit."*

"OK, Houston, we've had a problem here." ... as the often misquoted communication from Apollo 13 put it. And I think we can agree that it wasn't and isn't just in Houston.

I know I never digress (much), but as we speak, the Democrats in Congress are purportedly aiming to pass a bill that, among other things, would raise the minimum wage all the way up to $15 per hour, as many of them promised in their 2020 campaigns. Oh, goody!

But, um, what happened? Oh my! The currently proposed legislation would boost that wage to $15 *by 2025 at the earliest.* That's what got shot down yesterday. And not by liberals who thought it too stingy. No damn wonder people come to believe their votes don't count.

Back to our story ...

Mel loves to freak out new employees. (I somehow think

I've told this story before, but can't locate it just now. However, given the sales figures ... well, I can be pretty darn certain this is new news to most of you.)

Here's how.

Which I've got to confess caroms me off it in an entirely different direction, so back to Mel in a few.

“Here's how,” was my Dad's favorite toast. I never really understood it as a child, but, just now, abruptly, I got it.

Dad's “toast” was presumably a fallback to something from an earlier era. Right? How do you drink a shot of bathtub gin that very well may kill you due to its incautious distillery?

“Here's how!”

So Mel, introducing a new hire to the ins and outs of the fried chicken biz, would take said newbie to the deep fryer, drop some frozen chicken in the bubbling fat, and then, having wetted his own hand and arm at an adjacent sink, reach into the roiling oil and pull out a leg, thigh or wing. *Voila!*[113]

I know some will doubt this, but in absolute and utter fact, this is a trick your author's friend, actually an in-law at one point, pulled. Repeatedly. Of course, it wasn't Mel who is a fictional character first encountered on page 76 of the current volume, but it is a true story about a real chicken restaurant manager. Seriously. A wet hand, plunged into boiling grease, can emerge unscathed if the chicken was frozen and still cold. (But don't try this at home. Or if you do, it's on you, not me. This per my legal team's advice.)

Meanwhile, Doug? In case you ever read this, I'm not meaning to paste you with Mel's unfortunate disposition. You are not a model for this character in anything other than the boiling oil trick.

That out of the way, what do we know, or what can we learn about Mel?

He's a gem as fast-food managers go. Really truly. He's flexible regarding hours, working around the kind of family issues that so many worker bees confront, even filling in when kitchen help have an abrupt conflict like a court appearance, or a debilitating hangover, or simply need some “me time” due to the exigencies of life in late-stage capitalist society, and just generally making employment possible for folks who, frankly, are always at the bottom rung and sometimes slipping.

But. And isn't there always a “but?”

---

113 Yes, French!

But he is incredibly, insanely, intolerant of anyone who deigns to wear a Baby Yoda® tee.

You can immediately see the conflict, can you not?

Baby Yoda® tees are, like, the "big thing" just now, and while employees get the message on day one, customers are a whole 'nuther ball of ... I was going to say "wax," which is kind of a standard figure of speech, but in the current climate they are more accurately a whole 'nuther ball of COVID-19 aerosols just waiting to escape if the mask were to fall away.

So, just the other day, a young woman stepped up to the counter at the chicken restaurant, which I think I've failed to mention is operating out of the location formerly occupied by the Slick Wiccan Chicken® operation we read about on page 54, which made us all hungry for a bite [Wool of bat? Bring it!] and she was wearing a Baby Yoda® *face mask!*

Mel was instantly seething, peering out through the food slot between the kitchen (where he was supervising the fry-cook) and the sales area (where his underpaid but loyal front crew were scurrying to take and fill orders). His face grew red. His eyes were bulging. His hands were shaking. I think I even heard him growl.

What he desperately wanted to do was to roar out the side door, circle the building, come in the retail entrance, grab that unknown woman by the arm, turn her around, and rip that thing off her face! How dare she? How dare she? In his restaurant?

But no. He took a few deep breaths and reminded himself that in so doing he might very well expose himself to the COVID-19 aerosols mentioned just four paragraphs back, knowing as he does that anyone who'd wear a Baby Yoda® mask was more than likely to be the sort who is going out to bars and partying with large groups of friends and otherwise carrying on in non-socially responsible ways, and thus is practically a Typhoid Mary® in this time of cholera.

She, he realized, was a ticking super-spreader bomb, and the best course of action was to get her food out as quickly as possible and send her packing. And just like that he let go of his Baby Yoda® repulsion in favor of personal safety, at least in this instance. Gut feelings of this nature are extremely resistant to *abandonner,* and I think Mel should be applauded.

Don't you?

Lost at Long Last

I fear I've painted a rather one-dimensional portrait of Mel in the past few pages, and the feeling that this was unfair has plagued me for almost ten minutes. So we're going to circle back here and broaden our look at our *chef de poulet.*

For starters, and I know this will raise your opinion of the gentleman no end, he doesn't presently golf and never has. See? You like him better already. Dylan? "Nuh-uh."

Let's see. Oh, also, like the "good roomie" described on page 76, he is prompt with his share of the rent, does the dishes more than seldom, vacuums and so on and so forth. To take him up another notch in your esteem, he recognizes that he is in a higher income bracket than Leonora, given that she's in the early stage of her entrepreneurial career and deems that "his share" share of household costs is rightly larger than hers.

I can tell that some of you would kind of like to be his friend at this point, despite his foul temper regarding Baby Yoda®.

You could just drop by the restaurant some afternoon—after the lunch rush and before dinner, leaving your B Y® gear at home, of course.

Then too, and maybe you've noticed this when driving by, he talked the building owner into installing a solar hot water system on the roof. Restaurants use a lot of hot water, you know. And see again? He's really a good egg, as is the landlord, cutting the carbon footprint of the enterprise significantly.

Oh, and another thing, he's diverted some of the advertising dollars he's accorded by corporate to supporting a community radio station here in town! Whoo-eeee! Didn't see that coming, did you?

And here comes the clincher. Are you ready?

Like others among the population in the present volume, he owns an obsidian knife! He had it mounted in a glass-fronted case and has it displayed on a bookshelf ... which lends a further clue to his fine character. Yes, yes, he has books! And even reads!

But now you're thinking I'm exaggerating, and perhaps over doing this knife thing. "Where," you're asking yourself,

"Where on earth did Mel, an average *maître de poulet,* come up with a Mesoamerican artifact?

"Here's how!" as Dad used to declare.

Ned is Mel's brother. You know, the archeological anthropologist? Who collects such things? This particular knife was a birthday gift.

Which makes you wonder. If Mesoamerican culture is Ned's field, and a collection of volcanic glass cutlery is his particular "thing," wouldn't he be somewhat loathe to give up what might surely be an important part of his *œuvre?*

You've hit the nail on the head!

Let's take a closer look at said artifact, and then, in the manner suggested at the start of many an essay test: compare and contrast.

Is this, in fact, a Mesoamerican *souvenir?*[114] The correct answer is, "No." [Which is *not* the sort of short answer your teacher hoped to read in the above-mentioned essay test.]

What then? Did Ned give his brother a fake? If its the thought that counts, what kind of thought does that suggest? Does he not like his bro? Was it an act of ill will?

How quickly we leap to conclusions. Sad.

It is a real obsidian knife, and an old one, but here's the catch: it is a *Hawaiian* artifact. It's the kind of implement used to filet mahi-mahi or slice pineapples, not the kind used to excise beating hearts from sacrificial virgins, and so is of diminished interest to a man in Ned's line of work. A specialist can cover only so much ground. And as dear old Blaise Pascal used to say, *"Le cœur a ses raisons dont la raison ne sait rien."*[115]

Oh, he still admires the handiwork of the islander who chipped this thing from a formation of black glass, and he was appreciative when a cousin sent it his way, thinking, as the cousin did, that an obsidian knife is an "obsidian knife." But ... nay, nay.

Meanwhile, although Ned has told Mel whence the artifact, Mel likes a lurid story as much as the rest of us. So when he has friends over he allows that his *tchotchke*[116] *could* have been used to excise a virginal heart. [!!!!!]

Eyes have been known to widen, though on some visitors the excitement is quite lost. *"Le cœur a ses raisons ..."* Etc.& Etc.

---

114 Fifteen French words on one page! *Magnifique!* (No, sixteen!)

115 And what's true of the heart is very likely true of the Mesoamerican obsidian knife-wielder. Am I right?

116 Yiddish!

Confession

Confessions come in different flavors, as I'm sure you've noticed over the years. There's your plain vanilla variety, in which a friend might say something on the order of, "I've got to confess that those shoes you've got on look utterly ridiculous. Is someone paying you to wear them?"

Your feelings may be a little hurt, but that sort of admission is kind of off hand and may even be said in a joking manner. Perhaps you both laughed afterward, though it wouldn't much surprise us if you slept poorly that night.

"What did she *mean* by that? Isn't orange the new black?"

Then there's the secret confession told only in a whisper to the priest hidden in the other half of the phone booth. This is voluntary, at least to a degree, since after childhood it's a matter of free choice governed by one's fear of hellfire and strange belief that if hellfire actually exists then imparting secrets to a possible pedophile will get you a ticket to heaven. In terms of "flavor" this probably qualifies as *habanero* or *jalapeño*.[117]

During my grade school years there was a Cub Scout® in my Den who attended the local parochial school. He was the source of my first exposure to "bad" words and sexually loaded jokes. I knew they were at least "off-color," and one day asked Bobby about it. Did he feel guilty about the stuff he told me?

"No. I go to confession every week."

It made me wonder if the Father Confessor shared the jokes with his cohort. Some were pretty funny, at least to my previously innocent ear.

That sort of Catholic® confession was taken to its logical extreme during *l'Inquisition espagnole®*[118] when fear of hellfire proved insufficient to inspire voluntary conversion or admission of belief in heliocentrism and whatnot.[119] The rack, the iron maiden, the cat-o-nine-tails, water boarding and actual fire often

117 Spanish! Which will shortly lead us to the next variety.

118 I know, I know: This is French, not Spanish. Whose Inquisition was this anyway?

119 Though, post-confession it is alleged that Galileo muttered, "Eppure si muovono ancora," or something to that effect—in Italian!

proved persuasive. When your arms and legs are bound tightly to a stake, with oil soaked straw mounded up around your feet and the henchman is advancing with a flaring torch ... lips loosen!

One rather supposes that his devout Catholicism® had some influence on former Supreme Court Justice Antonin Scalia when he said he didn't see anything in the Constitution that prohibited the torture of detainees for the purpose of getting information. Scalia once told a BBC® interviewer that torture would be unconstitutional if it were inflicted as a form of *punishment.* (Italics mine.) Justice Scalia fit his legal tent peg squarely in the gaping round maw of the Inquisition®.

[One rather wonders, does one not? Is this the sort of thing Scalia would have offered up to *his* confessor? "Forgive me Father for I have sinned. I lusted after the chunky soprano at the opera the other night, I was a bit of a glutton at a restaurant before the show, I've probably been a little too prideful this week —regarding my brilliantly stellar legal opinions—and, oh, right, I approved of torture as a tool of government."]

["It happens to the best of us, my child. Meditate on Pope Lucius the Third. Forty days of prayer ought to fix things."]

You see, if your intentions are good ... well, then, torture is good as well. Inmates at Guantanamo just don't know what's "good for them," is all.

Such confessions, naturally enough, may be false. Duh. But following Scalia's whip-smart logic we can carry this forward to a reasonable conclusion. Intent: good. Torture: good. *Ipso facto:*[120] false confessions are good as well.

[It's kind of sad the way American military jurisprudence spoiled the word "waterboarding." When I was a youngster I waterboarded at the beach on the Atlantic coast quite often, running and jumping on a round or bullet-shaped piece of plywood and skimming in the tidal wash. Now if I tell someone "I used to waterboard," the person is apt to look at me strangely and back away. But I digress. Sort of.]

Isn't this story supposed to be about confession, and given the general tone of the present volume, expected to be in some way humorous? Right you are.

So, since we've entered the "legal realm" with that chit-chat about Scalia, let's pick on Judge Laura Marsh Green. Recall that she was presiding when the alleged *Noblet*® nabber was convicted by a jury of her peers on page 36.

120 Latin! We are feeling so worldly!

Gotta say that trial was a tough one for Judge Green. You likely noticed that we didn't indicate what *her* opinion was regarding the accused. That is as it should be. In a jury trial it is up to the supposed perpetrator's supposed peers to pronounce and then for the judge to hand down the appropriate punishment.

But, take it from me, I know her pretty well and she was inwardly shaking her head. She's seen a lot in her years on the bench and that young man who claimed his now notorious *Noblet*® was nabbed didn't strike her as "aboveboard." Green was not in the least surprised when the case was thrown out on appeal and Cappy Thornsen subsequently charged with false witness, which I don't think we mentioned upslope.

We might want to consider here, that, for the ancient Hebrews, anyone caught lying during their testimony could be forced to submit to whatever punishment would have been imposed upon the accused—even including death. "*Falsus in uno, falsus in omnibus*"[121] as the lawyers sometimes like to quip.[122]

In any event, Green threw the book at Cappy for his perjured testimony and he enjoyed several days in the local hoosegow, which his neighbors back home enjoyed even more, since they were spared the usual early morning squealing from the unstolen *Noblet*®.[123] Oh, and he was fined forty Big Bens and court costs. [First offense.] Guess he learned his lesson!

But we wanted to get back to Judge Green and her implied confession—implied between the title of this story and our selection of Her Honor as the subject herein.

Laura—we'll use her first name now that we're digging into her personal life—decided to study law when she was in junior high! That's pretty early in life to have made such a serious career choice and then stuck with it.

She made her mind up after watching the film version of *To Kill a Mockingbird*®.

We'd guess that most girls her age would more likely have identified with Scout, the young woman who's the narrator of that tale. But nope. She saw herself in Gregory Peck's character, Atticus Finch, an upright defender of the wrongly accused. "Call me Atticus!" she'd told her stuffed animals. Thus, her life's course was charted.

---

121 Latin again! Gee whillikers! And this is genuine lawyer talk!

122 Or, as they say in Hebrew: שקר בדבר אחד, שקר בסך הכל

123 Somewhat surprised one of them didn't use the opportunity to nab The *Noblet.*

She dated through high school and college but held back, not wanting to get too "serious" because she had her eye on a higher prize. Then came law school and editing its journal, clerkship for a lower court judge and several years as a public defender. Ever on the side of true justice! That's our Laura!

Finally she ran for a judgeship and won on the first try! This isn't often the case for those who leap into the political arena, but she has a winning smile, dimples too, and was able to articulate her legal views in ways that voters could understand. Anyone would be more than willing to be adjudicated by such a paragon. Anyone good, that is.

Bad eggs were in for a licking, which sounds awful. (Don't lick bad eggs at home, OK?) But, a fair and impartial licking, to be clear. Laura could and does mete out punishment with the best of them. [To the worst of them, obviously enough.]

"But to what has she or should she or might she confess?"

Glad you asked.

I'm entirely certain it isn't a felony. That's not in her *répertoire*. She really is a stickler regarding the law, in which case I think we could decide that it isn't even a misdemeanor, although perhaps that wouldn't dead-end her legal career—if it happened before she was 18. But no, not that either.

Just so you know she's not all "goody two shoes." She did get a speeding ticket once, driving through a small town in South Carolina that was practically the definition of a "speed trap." The local government leaned heavily on traffic fines for supplementary funding and had intentionally permitted a shrub to grow up in front of a speed limit sign. So she was nailed doing 40 in a 25 zone. Oh, the injustice!

That definitely did not go down well with our protagonist! Partly due to that experience she is finely attuned to such in the cases she hears. When there's even a whiff of police misconduct she's all over the cops like a rash! Honestly, if you find yourself in a legal snarl due to no fault of your own, you want your team of lawyers to draw her as your judge. She has a deep respect for innocence when it can be established.

On the flip side, however, if you know you're guilty you probably want your legal team to steer the case elsewhere. She holds everyone to her own high standards and she's a book-thrower if there ever was one! Practically a shot-putter as book-throwers go, with the heavy hand and the long arm often attributed to the law.

But it's high time we got back to her "guilty little secret." I think, given what you've learned about Laura up to this point, you've probably developed a fairly high opinion of her. You're perhaps also thinking she'd not be the life of the party, a little "too goody-two-shoes," so to speak, and that's not wrong. Then again, she isn't invited to many parties. Judgeship intimidates a lot of people, even the generally law-abiding, for fear some lapse in behavior at a social get-together will come back to bite one in the butt in some unforeseen future contretemps. [Don't pass that reefer to Laura!] So what can it be?

Aha! And let it be said right now that I am placing myself at some measure of risk in passing this along. I mean, I could end up in her courtroom myself someday, and if she finds out I told you I could easily end up doing hard time for something as simple as art theft. [In the Picassoesque sense[124] we discussed at some length in the phenomenally prescient volume *Seize You on the Dark Side of the Moo,* (Brave Ulysses Books, 2019).[125]]

So putting my future in jeopardy, and taking a deep breath, here goes.

Her Honor Laura Marsh Green is positively *titillated*[126] by the misfortunes of the rich and famous. She admitted this to me while you were thinking about Charles Mann on page 73, during a sidebar conversation when she allowed me to approach the bench.

She actually giggled.

Here's the thing. She has a P.O. box at the downtown post office which she rents under her mother's maiden name: i.e., "Marsh." Just L. Marsh.

She only retrieves mail there early in the morning and only when there's no one else in that section of the building.

That's where she picks up her subscription copies of *The National Enquirer®* and *Star®* magazine.

After she's savored every last delicious detail about movie stars, politicians and even aliens, and reports of real vampires stalking Hollywood® and the Village®, she tears off the address labels and recycles the papers in an anonymous public place.

In addition to what we can agree is already a profoundly powerful confession, she admitted to me that in doing all this she really feels naughty.

Very. Very, very, very naughty. [Sigh.]

---

124 "Great artists don't borrow, they steal."

125 We haven't paused for a commercial break for quite a long while.

126 Italicized for emphasis. If it were French it would be *titillé.*

Sweet Surrender[2]

By rights this should be Sweet Surrender[1], and the previous iteration (page 69) should have been Sweet Surrender[2] but I write this stuff down in the order that it emerges from the background noise or the fog. It's just the way I roll. Deal with it.

You see, Sarah McLachlan recorded her song in March of 1998, whereas John Denver delivered his ballad back in 1974 and had reached his date of expiry in October of 1997. So he *never heard* (emphasis mine) her version. Not only were the two songs separated in time but the two songwriters were distant in both physical and what we in the '60s called "head" space.

Sarah is Canadian. Denver was a product of Roswell, New Mexico, which raises more questions than the U.S. government is prepared to answer. What exactly was going on in Roswell in 1943? What were they hiding?[127] For that matter, what are they smothering now?

McLachlan was and is kind of meta.

Denver would never have penned:

"I've crossed the last line
From where I can't return
Where every step I took in faith betrayed me
And led me from my home."

You see? He was a lot more literal. Later more littoral, as we shall shortly see. By the sea, by the beautiful sea.

"Lost and alone on some forgotten highway,
traveled by many, remembered by few.
Looking for something that I can believe in,
looking for something that I'd like to do (beat beat) with my life."

I think we can be pretty sure he wouldn't have added

127 Reminding us (does it not?) of the astonishing tale "Sally's Fourth" in the often overlooked masterpiece, *Can We Have Archaic and Idiot? 2,* BUB, 2009. Ask your local indie bookseller or, for that matter, your local indie *used* bookseller. (All booksellers are, of course, "used.")

something like McLachlan's "It doesn't mean anything at all."

The only extant videos of Denver playing his song are from live performances and thus very straightforward. Man with guitar. Sings. As mentioned upslope, McLachlan's video version is, at minimum, strange. Yes, I think that's the right word, although, in fairness, that's long been the general direction.

Sixteen years later Lady Gaga's "Surrender" video went from McLachlan strange to "exceeding strange."[128]

Also, while the lyrics are largely unintelligible and unavailable online, there doesn't seem to be a lot of sweetness involved in the Gaga *assemblée*.[129] But I digress.

What got me started on this "Sweet Surrender^2" thing was laughing out loud when I mentally rearranged Denver's lyrics. [Someone has to do this work. And as noted way back on page 13, at the very beginning of this mess, I'm basically a sacrificial lamb when it comes to doing what needs to be done. Critics? Prepare your metaphorical obsidian daggers! I am strong—if not virginal.]

I was humming his "Sweet Surrender" and thinking, "Like a bird in the water, like a fish in the air," which is—as you immediately understand even if you've never heard the song—backward. Except after I laughed I realized that, in reference to Mr. Denver, *that isn't funny*. (Italics mine.) He died in the Pacific Ocean, we might say "littoraly," when the "bird" he was flying hit the water.

Now, I will admit, and such an admission being part of the subtext of the current volume, ever since October 12, 1997 [Four days before my birthday: hint hint.] [Day of the month, that is: I was 47 that year] ... ever since, I have believed, without any significant evidence, that it was a suicide. Well, a little evidence. Witnesses said the plane flew straight into the drink, and my thought was that if he were, say, running out of fuel, he surely would have tried to land on the plane's belly. At least affording himself time to climb out and swim.

And speaking of drink, he'd been doing too much of it, with multiple DUIs, and his pilot's license had been revoked. "Maybe he was morose," came to mind. Drunk and despondent . "Over and out."

But, as is my wont when penning (pixelating?) these fabulous tales, given that this story was going to involve Denver, I

128 Also Gaga puts more skin in her game. Rather, less fabric, except when she puts a lot more fabric in. "Nearly naked" is part of her brand.

129 French again. We're sort of back on track.

looked him up on what G.W. Bush liked to call "the internets."

Denver was sober when he died, and it turns out that it was almost certainly an accident caused by the design of the plane he was flying that day. It was an experimental model that evidently hadn't been thought through very carefully.

A word to the wise here: Don't fly a plane that hasn't been thought through *very* carefully. Say a Boeing 737 Max, to pluck one "out of thin air"—to coin a phrase.

See Denver's plane required switching from one fuel tank to another when the first was running low. Two problems here, and I think you'll agree that these are pretty serious and not well "thought through:"

1.) The fuel gauge was located *behind* the pilot's seat. He actually had to use a dental mirror to see it.

2.) The lever used to switch tanks was located there also.

!!

Not only that, but in order to reach the lever a pilot needed to unbuckle and turn a full 90 degrees to reach the damn thing, and in that position, straining to get hold of it, the natural tendency would be to apply pressure on one's right foot which would have pressed the right rudder pedal causing the plane to yaw and nose up, which, it turns out, is what witnesses had seen immediately before its precipitous dive.

So John Denver was not surrendering to depression, he was depressing something which kind of surrendered him to the consequences. His surrender in the song stands. In it he was lyrically surrendering any need to know what the future looked like, saying he was content to have the road lead where it might.

Maybe if he'd seen it coming he would have ... um, I don't know.

An odd thought: McLachlan's video depicts her running over herself while driving. Denver "ran himself over" while flying.

But, as ever, that isn't what this story is about. I just thought you'd want to know the result of this morning's deterined sleuthing.

No, indeed. We're going to have a heart-to-heart about someone else who surrendered, putting me in mind of my departed friend Philip Bowditch's favorite James Thurber story, "If Grant Had Been Drinking at Appomattox." Heh heh.

However, Delbert Hunter is our current "person of interest," a fellow we last met when he was defending the falsely accused purloiner of that pesky piece of poorly and peculiarly played instrumentation: the noble *Noblet®*.[130]

I wouldn't want you to leave this collection with the impression that Del[131] was a bad lawyer, despite his defense effort having failed in the original trial. After all, he was correct and did his very best to rescue his innocent client from the infamy of being labeled a common clarinet thief. Truth be told, conviction of the innocent is an all too frequent outcome of American jurisprudence.[132]

Del's appearances on pages 36 and 38 were pretty one-dimensional, giving you no particular indication of what, if anything, he might at some point, past or present, have ceded or conceded or, given that he's a lawyer, *"concedendum."*

Lawyers love them a little Latin, doncha know?

What you may very well not have understood up to this point is that Del is a chess player! Guess that bumped him up in your esteem machine, did it not?

Oh my gosh, yes! He is astoundingly adept at chess. At 2 a.m. on any given night you'll find him duking it out with an opponent in South Africa or Vietnam, online of course. He's so damn good that he rarely has to concede. He even plays Armenians! [Renowned as the world's best!]

Also, he has two cats. Two! Moxie and Azulapanula.

Here at the cat ranch we *know* what that means.

So. Hmm. Your understanding of this person is, at this point, deepening, which, we can agree, is an important element of fictional development, but ... I regret to inform you that that's not part of this story. We're looking for some place where he has *had to concede* something that matters to him, personally, deeply. Right?

Chess, no matter how one frames it, is only a game.

[Like golf. Which, we have not forgotten, is *not* a sport.]

I mean, we obviously recognize that in cases like the *Noblet®* caper, and many others in the course of a legal career, he's had to concede that the "jury is right," or "within its rights." But, honestly, that's not particularly interesting. You win some, you lose some. Etc. [Some are rained out.]

I see a hand up. "Grant at Appomattox?"

You presumably know I don't appreciate interruptions,

130 Thornsen's horn.

131 All together now: "A hypocoristic!"

132 Setting me off, as per usual, with a Beatles® ear worm. "Dear jurisprudence, won't you come out to play?"

but on the flip side, I'm the first to acknowledge that "the customer is always right." I'm assuming for the sake of argument that you or someone who cares a good deal about great literature actually purchased this book. [Please don't say you stole it—and don't go bringing up Abbie Hoffman either.]

OK, in a nutshell: Ulysses[133] S. Grant, like John Denver, was a habitual drunk, though, living in a pre-automobile era, he had no similar track record of DUIs. So James Thurber, who was quite the wit, I think you'd agree—quite—penned a revisionist history in which Grant was completely soused when his *aide du camp*[134] roused him for the meeting with Robert E. Lee.

Grant drunkenly proceeds to surrender to Lee!

Hope you weren't drinking coffee just now. Leaves me gasping. Whooee! Gotta catch my breath.

Where were we? Oh, Del. What he gave up. [Forgive me if I sound a little distracted, by the way. Yesterday I received an e-mail that indicated I had fallen into legal trouble with Disney®. Disney®! I was informed that I had in some fashion infringed on a copyright in last summer's wild ride, *Waist Not, Want Knot.*]

[What? I spent a couple of hours poring over the text and was unable to find anything Disney®-related.]

Back to Del—a lawyer—which reminds me that I may now stand in need of such—and his big sacrifice. Ah, got it.

Del wrote an op-ed piece about corruption in the North Carolina General Assembly. Del's father, Delbert Garfield Hunter, Jr., read it and phoned the lad to complain that he was afraid one of his friends would mistake Delbert G. Hunter III for himself, in which case he would die of embarrassment. He thought the opinion piece was *that bad.*

Which was the straw that crippled the camel, and we needn't go into the back story here. But that did it.

Del took legal matters into his own hands and changed his name. He is now simply, and officially, Del[135] Hunter.

Guess that showed him![136] *[137]

---

133 *Not* the source of my publishing house moniker, BTW. This book biz is named for a wonderful, wonderful cat. You can read about him in the 2021 "soon-to-be bestseller," *Self-Evident: We Hold These Tooths.*

134 Speak more French! Speak more French!

135 Meaning that this is no longer a hypocoristic. For the record.

136 Whew! Just got an e-mail from legal at Disney®. They have no idea where the previous message originated. Bullets no longer being sweat.

137 When this happened to me I dropped the L. and III from Cecil L.

Drain Flies Don't Bother Me.

"Drain flies don't bother me, drain flies don't bother me, drain flies don't bother me, 'cause they belong to somebody."

"Apropos what?" I hear you asking.

Very good question.

I have a couple of drain flies that have been hanging around in my bathroom for months—not that I know them to be the same two. They all look the same.If you're unfamiliar with these little boogers, they are BB-sized black bugs with over-large wings. I'm pretty sure I had never seen one before this winter. Certainly I'd never noticed one.

So I dragged out *The Audubon Society Guide to North American Insects and Spiders®* to discover who or what had invaded my domestic haven.

It turns out they are harmless, carry no foul diseases, and bother the dickens out of some people just by being there.

Not me.

Oh, and who they belong to?

My resident spiders, natch.[138]

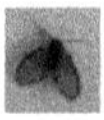

(Actual size.)

[And I do realize that this is totally silly. But I'm not afraid to let people know that I am not always the cerebral and deeply serious person I come off as to most readers of my soon-to-be National Book Award®-winning literary production.]

Bothwell III. Been plain old Cecil Bothwell ever since.

138 Speaking of which, in the three days since I composed this little "ditty" both drain flies have fled. Found one in a spider web. My theory is that drain flies "know" when they're not wanted and only stick around if they're not.

Expunge

This, I think, is another sort of "cede" entirely. Tell me if you think I'm missing the mark. Having something "expunged," from, say, *your* shady record [you know who I'm addressing here], is "something" someone else very clearly didn't want to see happen, or that "someone" wouldn't have recorded it in the first place.

Youthful folly, say, or more or less "serious" trouble at a tender and truly innocent age, that could reflect badly on you when you eventually apply for law school, for example, or for security clearance when seeking a night clerk job at a 7-Eleven®. Extortion, fraud, tax evasion, purse snatching, grand theft auto and vehicular homicide* ... the kind of things all of us do from time to time before we reach, say, 25? When our brains are finally congealing into something like an adult form, that is? We deserve, in the just- and fair-minded world that we are desperately trying to create [of late], to erase those childhood escapades from the permanent record. Do we not?

We do!

Glad to have cleared that up.

As we well recall Thomas Wolfe reflecting on that urgent, transitional period in life in his novel *Of Time and the River:*

> "The song had for him the fatality of something priceless, irrecoverably lost, full of that bitter joy and anguish we can feel at twenty-four, when the knowledge of man's brevity first comes to us, when we first know ruin and defeat, when we first understand what we have never known before: that for us, as for every other man alive, all passes, all is lost, all melts before our grasp like smoke; when we know that the moment of beauty carries in it the seeds of its own instant death, that love is gone almost before we have it, that youth is gone before we know it, and that, like every other man, we must grow old and die."

Right?

Right.

Here we're going to circle back to Officer Jeff Hansen. I

realize that he was kind of a bit player back there on page 28, so his name might not be "household" quite yet, but then the fat lady hasn't sung up to now—as the saying goes—which is, IMHO, a pretty weird saying.

How is it that sportscasters who, as a general rule, have never, never been within a shot-put throw—let alone a free throw—of an operatic production, offer up a referent to plumpster *Brünnhilde* when reporting on a football game?

For that matter, how is it that "your author," who is actually repelled by operatic sopranos, happened to interject the phrase in the paragraph up top? Good question. Lord knows.[139]

But we were considering Officer Hansen.

Those of us who've known him for, lo, these 67 pages are reasonably astonished that he was hired by the APD in the first place. What kind of background checks do they do? Anyway?

Knowing my readers I'm reasonably sure that as soon as his name popped up back there in the car theft investigation, you did a Web search on DuckDuckGo® to find out just exactly who this Hansen character is. I mean, it took him a long damn time to show up at the scene of the crime in question.

Forty-five minutes, to the site of a car theft?

What gives? (gave?)

Is our Officer Hansen routinely late? Does he, say, stop for a donut en route to the scene of a heinous crime? Was he parked under a shade tree texting on his iPhone® with his *amante?* Or playing Angry Birds® on said cell?

[Per cops and donuts. It's regrettably true that while I struggle to keep "making things up," the past haunts me like what's-his-name's *madeleines*. So, a quick flash-back. High school date night. Took my sweetie to a theater in downtown Orlando. Have no recall of the flick that figured in this frame—*Dr. Zhivago*?—but ... heading for home, going north on Magnolia Ave., the one-way companion to southbound Orange Ave.—the "main drags" in the latterly Disney®fied burg—I stopped at a red light. A cruiser with light-bar beacons flashing roared past us. Then another, then another, then another. "Oh my," I might have said. "Something's doing!" And a mile, or less, or more, later as we proceeded into Winter Park, we passed a Dunkin' Donuts® and saw at least seven cop cars parked and a cluster of officers inside drinking coffee and presumably "donuting."]

139 Irony. Humorous.

[I swear, you really can't invent this stuff.]
[And, I would testify in court, I am not.]

I'm absolutely certain you didn't learn anything about our subject's past crimes online, because, as suggested in the story title, Hansen's record was "expunged." You can't even find anything using the Wayback Machine®, since his particular mischief went down in the days before the military-industrial complex set the internets loose upon the globe. (The Kraken! The Kraken!)

This means, as you've surely realized, that few know about the incident, and fewer are willing to show-and-tell, meaning that I am very likely your only available source.

Wherein the publisher's [*mien*] legal team has given us [*nous*] pause.

Pause.

Um. Hmm.

It seems that while Jeff Hansen is an "officer of the law," he is not, in that capacity, deemed to be a "public figure."

"Why does that matter?" you thoughtfully query.

What my legal team has explained to me just now is that if I make assertions of illicit behavior concerning a non-public figure—no matter how horrendous—and you'll just have to trust me on this—horrendous!—and at age four—4!—absent corroborating testimony or physical evidence—buried I'm certain—I could be sued for libel.

So.

Never mind.[140]

140 See * on page 94. Hint, hint. Involving a tricycle, no less. A tricycle! You'd hardly think such a thing possible. But, then, there's this: If you drain your crystal wine glass (go ahead, I can wait …), and hold it up, then release it to plummet to the cobbled patio beneath your Buster Browns®, it is possible, if very narrowly so, that it will land intact. What seems impossible is, in fact, possible. Just rare. Very rare.

Sneeze

A sneeze is a particular sort of cede whether it's in response to a snort of pepper or dust, a flash of sunlight, a spoonful of cocaine or an allergic reaction or a symptom of the common cold ... in each case a nearly irresistible and automatic exhalation.

I say "nearly" as versus "simply" because if I said "simply" you'd be thinking about that Robert Palmer® video with all the shimmying dancers that so inflamed the pop world in 1987. This is something I don't want to initiate at present. [And to think it was his first single release! With all those supermodels he'd met at the Kentucky Derby®! A first release making it to #2 on the Billboard Hot 100®! I can see it in my mind's eye even as we speak! Those women were hot, hot, hot!]

But, no, let's not go there.

"Nearly."

What I want you to think about when I use the word "Nearly" is a gripping story so-titled, a fascinating investigation of love and loss and electronic *sottises*[141]—built around the idea that, theoretically at least, if you half the distance between yourself and some sort of destination in each given unit of time, you will never actually get there—found on page 68 of the impishly titled collection, *Can We Have Archaic and Idiot? 2.*

That fun-fest actually emerged from a science class, years before, in about ninth grade. I'm pretty sure it was Mr. Meyer, but don't hold me to it. (Long time gone.) This "Mr. Meyer" used the expression "For all practical purposes," and one of the brighter lights in the room asked, "What does that mean?"

The response set us all to giggling.

He said, "If we lined up all the young women in this room on one side and all the young men on the other and you walked toward each other, halving the distance between the two groups every minute—as we have discussed—in theory you would never meet, but you'd be close enough *for all practical purposes.*"

[Emphasis his.]

---

141 Yes. Fr.!

I'd venture that your day is already measurably brighter simply for having read the previous paragraph!

[These days he'd probably be fired for offering that kind of thing to young teens.]

But we were talking "sneeze,"[142] were we not?

A "sneaky sneeze," the kind that catches one unawares, is, as suggested, nearly irresistible. Sure there's the one where you go "ah, ah, ah, ah ..." and you have time to put your index finger beneath your nostrils and squelch the incipient exhalation

But how often does *that* happen?

And, for that matter, do you really *want* to stop? Some studies have established that you can actually rupture an eardrum when you suppress a sneeze. Further, you can damage blood vessels in your eyes or nose! It can even collapse your lungs!

Words to the wise there. Words to the wise.

"Mr. Meyer," by the by, is the teacher I pictured when I first heard Tom Lehrer's song, "My Home Town." You know the verse:

"The guy who taught us math, who never took a bath,
Acquired a certain measure of renown,
And after school he sold the most amazing pictures
In my home town."[143]

Not that I mean to suggest that "Mr. Meyer" was either unbathed or vending porn. It was just his face that came to mind, perhaps due to the mild sexual innuendo in his theoretical lesson regarding "practical matters." Since I've let him get in here between the covers with us, I think I'll go ahead and assert that he did, in point of fact, bathe regularly. As for the "porn," well *that's* a conclusive leap, is it not?

Lehrer didn't say *that,* did he? No, *he did not.* It could have been pictures of songbirds or dragsters or Oriental rugs. There are many things one might find amazing, notwithstanding the well-known fact that there are photographs people used to pay quite a bit for, pre-internet, and other images for which people were less likely to shell out serious money.

"Psst." [Opens raincoat.] "Want some pictures of house

---

142 For the record: substances which make one sneeze are labeled "sternutatory," coming from the verb "sternutation," adopted into English in the 16th century from the Latin, *sternutationem.*

143 From the album,*Songs by Tom Lehrer,* Lehrer Records®, 1953

wrens?" [Point made.]

Back on track now. What flows from the title at this point is consideration of the phrase "Nothing to sneeze at." Back when this idiom was coined, perhaps in the 18th century, it seems to have come from the idea of turning up one's nose at something. But it's clearly a scramble in modern parlance. If there's nothing there, why would one sneeze? And in this time of cholera, if you're the kind of good egg I know my readers to be, you aren't sneezing at anything or anyone. You *are* wearing a mask, are you not?

The outflow of a sneeze can reach speeds of up to 100 mph, propelled by a contraction of the sternum![144]

The unmasked among us could, I think, in this time of cholera, quite reasonably, be charged with possession of deadly weapons.

Meanwhile, one of the upsides of wearing a mask is that when a sneaky snip of sternutation catches us by surprise there is really no time to stop the process, meaning that masking is good for your health as well as the health of those around you.

As we recall from that thrilling novel, *She Walks on Water,*[145] in the scene where Japanese protesters are challenging the slaughter of dolphins, we witnessed a fairly common practice among certain, mostly young, persons in that nation, who go masked at all times in public. [True fact.] This, years before the current pandemic, has probably spared many from COVID-19 infcction.

"Nothing to sneeze at," indeed!

But, honestly, my train of thought has wandered considerably since I began writing this exposition three days ago, and I don't now recall where it was headed. I really should have caught the muse by the horns or the tail in the moment.

Oh, well.

"She's so fine there's no telling where the money went."[146]

---

144 Which I've gotta say here, coupled with "sternutation" and the Latin, "*sternutationem,*" led me to believe that "sternum" came from the Latin. Didn't you think the same? But no, the Latin word (phrase, actually) for "sternum" is "*rursum indidem gulam.*" Odd, that. But educational.

145 Brave Ulysses Books, 2013

146 Robert Palmer, "Simply Irresistible," from the album *Heavy Nova,* EMI 1988

Superceded

I always feel jubilant when I reach this point in a clump of short fiction, as should you. For me, it means I'm halfway to the goal posts—the 200-page target which has seemed "right" ever since 1981 when I read Dick Perry's helpful guide, *One Way to Write Your Novel.*[147]

He suggested a very simple strategy. Pick a time of day and write two pages daily during that same time slot. You'll soon come to see that establishing a routine makes the process much easier. This turns "someday I'm going to write a book" into the real thing. Very quickly you'll discover that, rather than being a "chore," your feelings shift. On any day when the exigencies of life inevitably disrupt your new routine it feels like a loss, not a release.

It doesn't matter what you write, because you're going to edit it in step two. It doesn't matter where you start. Have a great middle scene in mind? Start there. Or write your "great ending" first. You can change it later (and almost certainly will.)

In 100 days you will have a 200 page manuscript! Almost magical! Then, over the next 100 days write the second draft, editing and rearranging as you go—a necessary step since during the first trimester you, will discover that characters have taken on "a life of their own" and some or much of what you thought was going to happen didn't, because they really couldn't have, or else you need them to have done something you didn't arrange for them to do back on page 36 in order to lend verisimilitude to what happens on page 197, and so forth. [Editing is always easier than writing, by the way.] Then, over the next hundred days you put together the final draft.

A whole book in less than a year!

Back in those pre-word processor days this used to involve a typewriter, and the second draft literally involved scissors and tape. [Went there, did that.][148]

Ever since then I've believed that 200 pages is a nice size

---

147 Writer's Digest Books, 1981

148 *Iliamna,* named for the Alaskan mountain in whose shadow the bad person in the book meets his just deserts. (Unpublished. Thankfully.)

for a book, and by setting that target have always known that there is an end in sight. Also, that it will prevent me from just rattling on until I'd wind up with a monster like David Foster Wallace's *Infinite Jest,*[149] which I feel certain very few people actually finished reading (*moi? non*). I mean, really? 1,079 pages?

That lands in the vicinity of the King James Bible®, which many at least *claim* to have read. That's possible, but at least with the Bible the potential reading audience is living in stark fear of hell. That's kind of a motivating factor for a readership.

Not so much with Wallace's effort.

Just this morning I finished reading Thomas Wolfe's *Of Time and the River,* which clocks in at 912 pages in its original hard cover edition, and truth be told,[150] it was a slog. A brilliant slog, but a slog. And further truth: I read it on an electronic reader, so my nose was never in serious jeopardy. (See below.) One step further: I read it in the course of doing some very serious historical research, the culmination of which, I'm certain, will surprise or alarm many.

For myself, I don't want to be guilty of fashioning a tome that could break the nose of someone who fell asleep reading in bed. I'm thoughtful about my readers' well-being.

Concerning which you've been wondering, "What's in it for me?"

For you? Savor the pleasant realization that there will only be about 100 more pages to slog through before you are presented with the most excellent opportunity to consider Book Club Questions. Think of this as a downhill ski run. Up to this point you've been riding to the top of the mountain in a chairlift. Now it's "Whoosh!" I hope you're feeling as relieved as I.

Now, to buckle down–even as you on the chairlift are unbuckling or buckling up—"Superceded."

I know that word has been troubling some of you for almost two full pages, imagining I meant to write "superseded," though I would hope that, by now, you'd have some feeling that I know what I'm about. But I get it. Always finding fault. [Sigh.]

To supersede is, of course, to replace something.

To "supercede" is to really, really give up. [And, yes, I made it up.]

That's what we're going to explore now, in the life and

149 Little Brown, 1996

150 As per my usual

times of Adam Gottsen, the detective we met on page 34. Recall that he and his partner, Jim Pernal, were all over the case of the nabbed *Noblet*® and while they were disastrously misled by the false accusation asserted, we note that they actually found a *Noblet*® in the possession of the accused, which looked pretty darn incriminating.

To be further fair, while they both had decades of experience as investigators they had never before dealt with a case involving a stolen clarinet, nor had either been in, say, a high school orchestra or jazz quintet, where they might have been exposed to a nice *Noblet*®. (Nor to France where they might have been to the capital of the *Alpes-Maritimes département* and there admired a *Nice Noblet*®.)(Pronounced "niece.")

Truth be told,[151] absent the noun following the French moniker, neither would have been able to guess what the *Noblet*® named. "A small knob?"[152]

"Some variation on goblet?"

"No blet? What's a blet?"

"Noble 'T'? Is that like Queen Elizabeth® or something?"

And so forth.

You, on the other hand, have now attained a certain *savoir faire,* and when someone in your circle sings the praises of a *Noblet*® you will henceforth be able to nod knowingly. "Ah, yes," you will mutter. "So true." Your heart will be gladdened.

Tra la.

For that matter, Adam and Jim have learned the same and can elevate their banter with their fellow officers when they're parked window-to-window in a grocery parking lot.[153]

Adam, as you've already inferred, had to really, really cede something that held great significance for him. That is, to use the word I've coined, he "superceded" said object. An object, we will now come to realize, by which he set great store!

---

151 By now you have come to understand my steadfast commitment.

152 Which, of course, would be a "knoblet" leading us straight back to the discussion of gnus and knowing and so forth in the hilariously funny story titled "Gnawing Desire" on page 68 of *Self-Evident: We Hold These Tooths* (Brave Ulysses Books, 2021) wherein we find the suggestion that it might be pronounced, "k-noblet."

153 Don't you wonder what cops talk about during those nose-to-tail chats? I've always imagined they're up to no good, taking their talk "off the air." But, I dunno, maybe just interested in seeing a friendly face for a change.

[The store that figures in the story is great, but in a different fashion. Yummy in the tummy comes to mind.]

To understand this we'll have to go back four years. Adam was looking into a case of thievery, a smash-and-grab from a candy store, a *chocolatier*. He didn't expect to find stolen goods, given that the goods in question were likely *en route* to the "National Trust."[154] But there was blood on the glass, and DNA has solved more than one mystery.

"Poor schmuck," he muttered. "Must have been really jonesin' for a marzipan."[155]

The *chocolatier,* himself, had been in a kitchen out back and hadn't even heard the glass shatter. It had happened pre-dawn[156] and there were apparently no witnesses.

After interviewing the owner, Adam was walking back to his squad car and happened to spot something glinting in the grass growing around a street tree, something sticking out between the trunk and the iron circle of the grate.

He bent closer. It looked like glass, only not like the broken beer bottle shards or head- or tail-light lenses one sees here and there on the city's mean streets. It appeared to be black glass and blade-shaped. Adam went down on one knee, holding his evidence kit in his left hand, and reached, but thought better, stood and walked to his vehicle to stow the kit and pull latex gloves out of the box. (He'd already shed the pair he used at the scene of the heist.)

Returning to the tree ...

"C'mon! C'mon!" I hear you thinking.

Patience. This is all leading up to *the* moment. The terribly exciting moment. It's critical to the story unfolding even as "you think," or "we speak," or whatever idiom suggests immediacy in your *argot.*[157]

So, please don't interrupt.

Returning to the tree he went down on one knee once again and reached for the object with his now-gloved right hand. He pulled the treasure slowly from its ... its what? Grave? Perhaps, but only one-half to two-thirds in, like your somewhat

---

154 Beatles® reference, see page 29. Regarding "flushing."

155 Which you probably think is French. But no. *Massepain.*

156 Reminding us of the burglars mentioned on page 66.

157 Italicized to indicate French. Since the pronunciation is essentially the same in English, we need to read this with a French accent in order to obtain the full and succulent flavor of this *moment dans le temps.*

jocular pal who says "one leg in and the other one ..."

"C'mon!"

OK, I'll cut to the chase. "Cut" being entirely germane in the present case.

"What the ..." Adam muttered. "A glass knife?" He wiped the object clean with the shop-cloth he'd been holding in his other gloved hand. "How odd."

Well, as you've already realized no doubt, what he was holding was an *obsidian*[158] knife with a carved horn handle! He didn't know *that* in the moment, but he did know it seemed pretty darn unusual.

That evening he took a picture of the thing and DuckDucked® an image search. "Wow! I have an *obsidian knife!*" he exclaimed, in an italicized half-whisper. "Gosh!"

Then, louder, to Dotty who was in the kitchen. "Honey, I have an *obsidian knife!*" (Italics his.)

It seemed pretty strange to him, as well it might to you, to have found such a treasure poking out of a tree grate in downtown Asheville. There's a regrettable shortage of volcanic glass in this portion of the continent. Hereabouts we're more into garnet, staurolite, kyanite, quartz schist, micaceous quartzite, calc-silicate rock, biotite gneiss, amphibolite, and phyllite—as you are surely aware. (But, seriously, aren't those names fun to say?)

Now, rest assured, this was a replica, not an actual neolithic tool. But it was still pretty darn cool! These things sell for hundreds of dollars. In no time at all he had mounted it on a wooden stand and placed it in a position of honor on his mantel.

Unfortunately,[159] or so it must seem, Adam and Jim are good friends, as are their wives, and so they "socialize." I don't mean that it's unfortunate to be friends, rather that the friendship proved to be a causal factor regarding the upcoming cession.

A few weeks later Jim and Nan were over for a barbecue with Rob and Mel and Dotty[160] on the Gottsen deck and Adam took the two couples into the living room to show-and-tell concerning his prize.

"Stolen goods," Jim announced, shaking his head.

"Really?" the other officer asked, crestfallen.

"Yeah. That pawnshop caper out on Patton. You weren't on that case. I'm all but certain."

---

158 I told you. They're stuck in here all over the place.

159 See footnote 64

160 Five hypocoristics in one sentence! Score!

You can see right there that this would lead to a pretty super cede. And so it goeth. Rather, wenteth.

"Crumbling"—continued from page 196.

I know I said Larry goes down there "every year," but of course he had to skip it during this "time of cholera." So he's really jonesing at this point. Plus, Lisa is willing to learn and he has a backyard pool! Plus, the backyard pool is very, very private and they can scuba nekkid! At night! [I told you they were in a "happy place!"] But we've wandered a little, haven't we?

We were going to explore Larry in a bit more depth, to understand his rich inner life, and here we've gone all *risqué*. [Appropriately enough, *en français*.] I apologize, sometimes my imagination runs away with me.

For one thing, Larry is a really thoughtful guy. Ps and Qs, remembers birthdays, phones his Mom pretty often. Lisa lucked into this one—reminding us that no ill wind fails to blow someone a bit of benefit.

For another, he doesn't golf, and if there's one lesson I hope you take away from these pages, it's this ... let's say it all together: "Golf is *not* a sport."

But what we want to dig into is "what makes him tick."

We're all the result of so much *sturm und drang,*[333] especially the *drang* part. So what we want to unearth is Larry's *drang*. Right?

This all goes back to an incident in eighth grade. [At least that's what he tells people. But as we've discussed on numerous occasions, people lie, particularly to burnish their personal reputations. Sure, a lot of the time we tell ourselves that we're sparing *someone else's* feelings, but a little self-examination is apt to tell us otherwise. A friend of mine once made a New Year's resolution to tell the truth for twelve months. Basically, I think what happened is she simply didn't say things aloud. She reports that it was a *very difficult year* and that she finally quit as Christmas approached and her young son was still in Santa mode. She decided not to disabuse him. Not so much to maintain his youthful fantasy as to not send him to pre-K—or whatever grade—with information that might well have caused conflict with other youngsters. Then, if I remember correctly, some other kid told him that Santa was make-believe. So much for good intentions.]

[Ran out of page again. There's more blank space on page 142.]

333 German!

Mislaid

That business with the backyard barbecue knocked around in the old noggin for a couple of days and here we are.

You recall Ellen and Don Fulton, no doubt. Ellen is the woman who rescued Don from the calamitous life he'd led as a bachelor.[161] What we didn't previously examine is how Don was able to afford his escapades "out west" back in the day.

Was he super-frugal, saving every cent in order to take time off for touring? No, he's kind of a spendthrift. Did he earn big bucks? No, that came later when he got the job we considered on page 41, you know, with the main office in Atlanta?

"How then?" you must be wondering.

Well, it seems he's what you'd call a "rich kid." Got rocks. His folks? Loaded. And here's where the barbecue comes in.

Don's parents were in town for a visit. Happily for him they live two states away, so they aren't always underfoot. Not necessarily happy for Ellie. Grandparents do a lot of baby-sitting if they're at all caring. At least they host Don Jr. every summer for a month, and the kid loves it, so that's something.

One evening the four adults were on the patio while Junior played in the yard. Don was grilling burgers on a three-legged, light-weight Weber®, and waxed reminiscent. "Whenever we're grilling I think back to our place in Ohio and that brick barbecue unit in the yard. The chimney seemed so wonderful to me when I was a kid."

"We still use it," the elder man[162] said.

His wife smiled and added, "Don Jr. likes it a lot!"

"Maybe, someday," her son mused.

Driving back to the northwest the couple talked about the son's sweet memory. "Why don't we hire a crew to build one for them while Junior is with us this summer? They're flying to Hawaii for two weeks. Wouldn't that be a surprise!"

"Linda,[163] that sounds great!"

---

161 See page 53 if you need a refresher.

162 I'm not using names here, since the grandparents are bit players and I think we've encountered plenty of givens already. No use confusing you.

163 Sorry. He said it, not me.

Linda and her husband made stealthy arrangements, hiring an architect to draw up plans, then locating a masonry contractor in Asheville and scheduling the job for the last two weeks in June, with strict instructions regarding the completion date. Having high-balled the price, the contractor, Bill Olsen, was more than willing to block in the time, regardless of other work he might be engaged in. It would only be a handful of days.

He wrote the address on his notepad. "19 Lookout. BBQ pit facing the slate patio. Finish on or before 6/26." No prob.

Only there was.

When the time rolled around, with Don and Ellie in Hawaii and Linda and her husband and Don Jr. off in the Canadian rockies, and Bill and his two employees headed to the job site, Bill couldn't recall if the address was on Lookout Rd. or Lookout Dr. He tried phoning Linda but no answer.

"OK," There was another way. He could go by both houses and see if anyone was home, then apologize if someone answered the door. "Oh, I must be looking for the other street."

He went to the road addy first, no one at the brick home, and a slate patio out back. That seemed right. On the other hand there was a dog looking out the window, barking. Wouldn't they have boarded a dog? Just to be sure he went to the other place where a week's worth of newspapers were piled up on the front porch. Another slate patio out back and a boy's bike locked to a rack in the rear vestibule. Linda had mentioned a grandson. This had to be it.

In short order they dug a rectangular hole, laid in some re-rod and poured the footing. Over the next two days they laid red brick to match the house and fire brick to line the firebox, installed an ash dump and a rear door for the bake oven, with an eight foot chimney to carry smoke up and away from guests and chef. A real work of masonry art.

A day later Bill happily deposited the fat check. Another job well done, and well rewarded.

I know you can see where this is going.

Tim and Penelope Morgan[164] were sure surprised when they returned home from their week at the beach. In retrospect, when Bill and Co.[165] built the second BBQ pit the check didn't seem quite as hefty. Mislaid indeed.

---

164 Sorry to complicate things. Maybe the Morgans will figure in some other story, so the names aren't completely wasted.

165 Sparing you two more names.

Degauss[166]

It's not a question of "Can you?" it's a matter of must.[167] Yes, it will become less attractive, at least for a while, but that's to be hoped for, not feared. Sure, attraction has its upsides, but there are drawbacks as well.

This bit of advice—much like my suggestion that you *not* follow in John Denver's footsteps (rather, flight path) in purchasing an airplane in which the fuel gauge and the fuel tank switch are, respectively, out of sight and out of reach for the pilot —will stand you in good stead. Someday you'll thank me.

But surely you've wondered, being one of my A-list readers,[168] how it is that the mulch you had delivered from the local stump-and-pallet grinding operation is free of nails. After all, you ponder, pallets are nailed together, are they not?

You're on the money!

I'm going to bring in Tim Morgan for a somewhat technical explanation in a few minutes, since he actually works in just such a business! [We didn't see that coming on page 107, did we?]

But first we need to step back or up and get a 30,000-foot view, the broad picture of the situation in question.

You get it. All the yard waste, the prunings, the bagged leaves, the trunks and roots of excised trees, the storm-toppled vegetation—all of it—needs to go *somewhere,* and what could be more appropriate than grinding it all into mulch? That's about as perfect a recycling loop as can be imagined.

I mean, I know you're a "non-apartment-dweller," else you'd not have ordered up a load of mulch, and so you have a compost pile out back, but you're hardly going to compost the tree that fell on your car during the last windstorm, now, are you?

Although, I ought to interject here—for the record—that Masanobu Fukuoka, the Japanese genius of agronomy, after years

166 Not to be confused with *Edgar Degas,* whose name I drop here given the obvious appeal that mentioning of an *artiste français* is likely to have, for say, National Book Award® judges.

167 And more about "must" anon.

168 As previously noted, you're past half-way to the goal posts at this point.

and years of experimentation, determined that the fastest way to build friable soil in poor agricultural land was to bury logs and plant daikons. Rotting logs become great topsoil in short order and daikon roots go deep into even the worst soil, both breaking it up and recovering minerals. Also, as Garrison Keeler used to say regarding Raw Bits®, "Heavens, they're tasty and expeditious!"

But the question emerges: "Why on earth are we grinding up pallets? Shouldn't they be reused?"

In a perfect world, of course.

But the problem is that an awful lot of stuff gets shipped on pallets from places to which we don't ship stuff back.

It's a lot like those 50-gallon juice containers that people turn into rain barrels. Juice gets shipped from South America, for example, and we don't have anything liquid for which there is a big market in the originating country. Sadly, shipping the empty containers back south is not economically viable in this era of late-stage capitalism. Perhaps in our Green future we'll be able to lade solar powered tankers with the empties. [A man can dream.]

Regarding which I would note, that while putting a 50 gallon container under a downspout seems admirable (and I have two myself), it is more a display of good intentions than a meaningful exercise. Say you have a guttered roof area that is 20' x 40', and a rainstorm delivers an inch of water. That adds up to about 500 gallons, rendering the filled container something like a drop in the bucket.

Then, of course, when you actually need water for the garden, you only have 50 gallons, which ain't much. To really benefit from rainwater catchment you need a tank that holds thousands of gallons and a pump. [Add that to the list on the fridge.]

At least, at least, you've kept the barrel out of the landfill, if temporarily, which is something.

So, anyway, some pallets do get reused, and in fact, some companies even charge a deposit in order to get them returned. These tend to be really sturdy units, used for, say, bags of cement. But a whole lot get ground up or, in worst-case scenarios, burned.

Here's Tim, to fill you in on the technical aspects of his corner of the market.

"Hi folks. Tim Morgan here, with Happy Valley Mulch®. Believe I was called in regardin' dealin' with hardware in the grindin' up of the damn pallets.

"Y'see, what we do is, well in the grinder, y'know, this big machine where we put the stuff in to chop it up fine, y'know, well there's a magnet. Powerful son-of-a-bitch, I mean. 'Lectro-magnet, akshelly, so's it can turn on and off. When it's on, I mean, you don't want nothin' steel in your pockets. No belt buckle neither, I mean, zipper on your fly's bad enough, makes your jeans puff out, but, I mean, you got a pocket knife in yer pants? You get too close to the grinder? Hell's bells! Yer askin' to be part of the mulch pile, y'know what I mean? I don't even like to think what'd happen. Real mess, is what an' I'd likely get the job a hosin' it down. The blood. Guts too, y'know. No thanks!

"Then, after—when we've done up the pile of pallets—we turn 'er off and have this big pile of nails. Y'see?"

Thanks Tim.

Before you readers distracted me from what I wanted to tell you, with all your puzzling and speculation about mulch and nails, what I really wanted to tell you involves Tim's better half, Penny, who works as a crane operator.

"Where?" [I hear you asking. And thanks for that, it helps move the narrative along.]

Why, at the scrap yard down by the river along the railroad! And here's the thing [and what a coincidence!] ... Penny's work involves a *powerful magnet* as well! Gosh! Maybe that's why they were *attracted* to each other? [Just kidding. But there's another coincidental connection. The nails from Happy Valley Mulch® go straight to Riverside Iron & Scrap®. Small world!]

When you're down there you see piles of construction aluminum over on one side, bins full of aluminum and steel cans, a loading dock to receive copper, brass, electric motors, wire, stainless and such, and out back a mountain of steel and iron that needs to be loaded into train cars. Penny operates a big crane with a massive electro-magnet on the business end, with which she hoists tons of magnetic metal from the mound over to the waiting gondola, then cuts the electric to release the load.

She's good at what she does and wears sound-deadening headphones on which she listens to podcasts.

"About what?" you ask, contributing once more to the narrative.[169][170]

---

169 See page 12.

170 No, I mean page 9. [Made ya look!]

And am I glad you asked! About wine-making! Penny is an oenophile and has been making and bottling her own vintages for several years. That's probably not a hobby you'd immediately think of when considering a crane operator, now is it?

Each fall she harvests grapes from the arbor in the backyard,[171] out behind the free brick barbecue grill we considered in the wry and thought provoking story "Mislaid," a few pages back, and she prepares her must[172] in a sawed-off juice barrel, generally mashing the fruit with what looks a good bit like an oversized potato masher.[173] [She actually made it herself out of a stainless steel microwave rack she found at the scrap yard. Clever as the dickens she is!]

The first couple of seasons the results were ... well, to be kind, OK ... as cooking wine. But between the podcasts and the practice she's becoming quite good, as amateurs go. "Drinkable" is, I think a fair assessment.

"How did she happen to become a wine hobbyist?" you ask, moving things along once again.

Well, that's what I've been trying to tell you for more than three pages.

When Tim and Penny bought the house there were already mature grapevines out back. The green-thumbed elderly couple who had moved out had lived there on Lookout Drive for many, many years. They'd finally decided they'd be better off in a retirement community and were fortunate to find one with a big communal garden, which somewhat dimmed the sense of loss in abandoning their longtime plantings.

Leaving what you've grown over decades has to be the hardest part of saying goodbye to the old homeplace. I mean to say, even that shmaltzy song "Honey," by what's his name. Um. Oh, right, Bobby Goldsboro. Even there. It made it to #1 on the U.S. charts and sold more than a million copies in 1968, and my theory is that the reason that happened is his mention of the tree right off the bat.

"See the tree, how big it's grown / But friend it hasn't been too long / It wasn't big." Then the part about how when she

171 And grows her own grapes! Wowza!

172 I told you we'd get back to it. (From the Latin *vinum mustum*, "young wine," and now you know.)

173 One time she did it with her feet, but although she is kind of pint-sized there isn't a whole lot of space to move around. We've got to give her credit where due, since she at least *experimented* with tradition.

planted it, it was "just a twig." [She dies alone, he's not home.]
[Insert pathos, or maybe bathos.]

Pretty much everyone can connect with that. Like when you revisit a childhood home, tree growth pops right out at you. Or tree absence. Or tree replacement. Or tree topping. (Grrrr! No. No. No. Don't top trees. Ever. Never ever.) And if you've ever lived in a place for, oh, a decade, say, well you've surely witnessed the changes as the twig you planted becomes a shade tree.

If Goldsboro had started out "See the *macramé*[174] she tied, two feet tall and three feet wide," it would have missed a lot of people, I think. Or, "See the *découpage*[175] she pasted, she was drunk and pretty wasted?" Nah. In order to sell a whole lot of records you need a hook[176] that a lot of people can identify with.

But, as those crazy Czechs so wittily quip: "*Postavit dům, zasadit strom, zplodit syna.*"[177]

Couldn't have said it better myself, though at this period of late-stage capitalism and climate crisis I'd go easy on the "*zplodit syna.*"[178]

Now, to get back to degaussing. As I said from the start, it isn't a question of "Can you?" it's a matter of must.

Demagnetization may not be for the weak of nerve, but it is a "thing." You can take that to the bank.

---

174 French!

175 Ibid.

176 As recently noted in the *NYT*® (3/15/21), pop music has subsequently shifted gears entirely. For decades the song form was verse/chorus, verse/chorus, but today it's hook, hook, hook, because artists are mostly paid per listen instead of per purchase. The more hooks in a song, the more likely a listener will stick around. A "listen" only counts in terms of income if it lasts more than 30 seconds, so like long-line fishermen* a clever songwriter needs to add as many hooks as possible.
"It doesn't mean much, it doesn't mean anything at all" per McLachlan.

177 Czech! Chalk up another world language!

178 "Have a son" for those few readers not fluent in the lingo.
*[This does not imply my approval of long-line fishing, BTW.]

Crestfallen

Paul Simon said it before Dr. Wardle,[179] but Dr. Wardle was quoted in the *New York Times*®. So there's that.

"This means that there is an interesting interaction between perception and cognition—our beliefs and prior experience can influence what we see. Or more accurately, what we think we see."[180] [so said Dr. Wardle.]

Isn't that the truth? A corollary would be "What we think we *don't* see," or inversely, "What we don't think we see." We're talking Tasmanian tiger (*Thylacinus cynocephalus*[181]) here, but many other things have been seen or not seen by many among us, as I'm sure you understand.

This recalls to mind what has to be a myth, though at this point in late-stage capitalism it would be difficult to prove. Some New Agey books have tossed around the idea that when European tall ships showed up in the Americas, or Australia, or wherever, the indigines couldn't see them because the concept of a large craft with sails and bearded white beings on deck singing sea chanties in three-part harmony was simply beyond their cognitive reach.

The root of that whopper seems to lead back to Joseph Banks, the botanist on Captain James Cook's 1770 voyage, who wrote in his journal that on several occasions as they sailed along the Australian coast, the fishermen, "seemd (sic) to be totally engag'd (sic) in what they were about: the ship passd (sic) within a quarter of a mile of them and yet they scarce lifted their eyes from their employment."

What such an observation actually illustrates, of course, is Banks' confirmation bias. In his frame the HMS *Endeavor*® was a BFD[182] and should have gotten the Aboriginals all hot and

179 Though Paul's reference point is music, leading to his version, "A man hears what he wants to hear and disregards the rest." ("The Boxer," Columbia, March 21, 1969, later included in the LP *Bridge Over Troubled Water.*) I don't know if he's ever heard a Tasmanian tiger.

180 *International New York Times,* 10 March 2021

181 Latin again! Just makes me smile.

182 "F" as in "fricking." This is intended for a General Audience.

bothered. But they were subsistence gatherer/hunter type folk, and "what's for dinner?" surely held more immediate interest than someone else's fancy-ass boat.

Banks was basically thinking, "Hey, look at us! We're so totally cool!"

In his recent book, *Useful Delusions: The Power & Paradox of the Self-Deceiving Brain,*[183] Shankar Vedantam suggests: "Our minds are not designed to see the truth, but to show us selective slices of reality, and to prompt us toward predetermined goals. Even worse, they are designed to do all this while giving us the illusion that we are seeing reality."

Seems about right to me.

When the Cook crowd *did* go ashore some of the locals came at them with lances, having no problem at all spotting their potential adversaries. Banks was, of course, unaware that Aboriginals had been engaged in trade with Makassars for hundreds of years. The traders sailed down from Indonesia, then carried goods from Australia to China and places in between. Back and forth. Sailboats were not a new phenom. There are extant Aboriginal cave paintings of sailing ships that predate Cook's visit by centuries, for heaven's[184] sake.

To Cook's credit, and Banks' as well, they didn't pull a *Cristobal Colon*[185] on the natives and take to chopping off hands and so forth, or helping themselves to slaves. They collected botanical specimens, drew maps, and spent a couple of months making repairs after the undauntless *Endeavor*® ran aground.

As far as I have been able to determine, Cook & Co.® never saw a Tasmanian tiger. [Perhaps such an animal was outside their cognitive framework?] We can be pretty sure they would have mentioned it in their logs. A yellowish dog-shaped animal with tiger-like striping on its rear half, front legs that could twist in order to grasp,[186] and, if it were a female, carrying youngsters in a pouch. Something like a carnivorous "'roo." Definitely a "We're not in Kansas anymore" sort of observation.

Hara Johnson thinks she has. Rather, thought she had.

When we last checked in with Hara she was terminating what might be called a "Dear John" phone call with Dennis

183 W.W. Norton & Co., 2021

184 A figure of speech. There is no heaven.

185 Spanish!

186 *Felis catus domesticus* can do this. *Canis lupus familiaris?* Nope.

Vernon.[187]

Tasmanian tigers have been "officially" extinct since the last "known" specimen, name of Benjamin, died in captivity at the Beaumaris Zoo® in 1936. While they had been driven to near extinction 2,000 years ago in mainland Australia, there were sightings there up until the 1830s, and the last shooting of a wild thacyline in Tasmania occurred in 1930. [Like ranchers and farmers and the wildlife regulators who support them in the slaughter of wolves in North America, Aussies created a cash bounty system aimed at exterminating their striped marsupial predator.]

Believers remain, however. "Sightings" occur. Camera traps are set. [Also fraudsters with Photoshop® ply their merry pranks.]

Not to mention "deep fakes," about which more anon.

So far,[188] present-day camera trap snaps have proven inconclusive for nonbelievers, and quite convincing to their opposite numbers. No one seems to have obtained a full frontal or a full profile, and the flash photos of moving creatures at night are pretty sketchy.

But traps have been laid for the unwary, and Hara is such. We saw evidence of this in her brief affair with our Demo Derby dummy Denny. What she saw in him I really can't fathom. Anyone unhinged enough to risk life and limb on a flat out gamble for a few hundred dollars? Well, well.

This is not to say that the event turned out badly for Mr. Vernon. He did net $400 and change, plus whatever he collected at the scrap yard for his dead ride. But that was nothing like a "sure thing." If he'd been T-boned, even inadvertently, with sufficient force he could have both lost his entry fee and his corporeality—not that he would have been concerned with the former if he'd suffered the latter.

The alternative being obviously worse.

Had he been permanently maimed *and* sacrificed the fee? We can see that the outcome could have been dreadful. [This was the line of reasoning that ultimately convinced my younger self to steer clear, for what it's worth.]

Yet, as we saw, Hara was cheering wildly for dumb Denny, and the pitcher of *piñas coladas*[189] is a sufficient explanation but

---

187 Page 47.

188 i.e. 5:27 a.m. EST, 12 March, 2021

189 Mm-hmm. Sp!

hardly a sufficient excuse.

To get back on track, Hara has always been hungry for the *rara avis*. A Dr. French told the *NYT*®, "The single most pervasive cognitive bias we all suffer from is confirmation bias."[190] If you really want to find the cryptid[191] you're searching for, you're more likely to find a given piece of evidence convincing.

For Hara it's come in phases.

There was her UFO period, then the yetis, a short trip down ivory-billed woodpecker-dom, a shorter dalliance with the Hollow Earth Theory [oh dear!], and a somewhat more enduring disbelief in the Flight 77/Pentagon scenario. She's still asking herself "Where were the wings?" [It seems the computer-generated reenactment she's watched several times has only just begun to work its way into her cognitive framework.]

The most convincing elements, IMHO, are the light poles that were knocked down as the plane swooped in. A missile would have had to dodge all over the place to make that happen.

Personally speaking, and being deeply reluctant to interject or digress as you've certainly come to understand by now, I'm still in my UFO frame. It all came to a head in 1978.

Oh, it's true that in the '50s there was a flurry of alien excitement. My best friend Doug [RIP][192] and I cut out newspaper photos and thumb-tacked them on a corkboard in my family rumpus room, together with clippings of articles and a world map which we stick-pinned with locations of "sightings." We were little Sherlocks whowere certain we could "solve" the mystery.

That was "what it was." But what happened in 1978 was an order of magnitude different. Say a Whopper® versus White Castle,® though more closely resembling a bunned wiener than a whirling burger.

Susan[193] and I had driven into Exeter, New Hampshire, to see a film. We were headed back out to our rented place in Fremont[194] at about 9:30 p.m. I was driving.

Ahead we could see an inordinately bright light. At first glance it appeared to be something like a new street light, but as

190 *International New York Times,* 10 March 2021

191 Viz: a creature that may or may not exist.

192 Irony. But sad-making. He reached his date of expiry at age 20.

193 See footnote 82.

194 Yes, the one with the ducks. Read all about the duck's misadventures in the title story in the quite amazing and rightly treasured collection, *Self-Evident: We Hold These Tooths,* BUB, 2021.

we drew closer it seemed to be too high up.

"Do you see that light?"

"Obviously, idiot. What do you think it is?"

"A helicopter?"

As we crossed a bridge over a 4-lane it was clearly a *very* bright object, and perhaps 200 yards further on I turned left on the road to our house, stopped the car and got out.

"What are you doing? Are you crazy?"

"Gotta find out what this is."

I looked directly up at a clearly physical object that radiated an intense blue-white light with a reddish glow toward one end. It was completely silent, hanging there about a full tree height above the surrounding trees. So maybe 120-160 feet up. As I stood there gazing, Susan's curiosity got the better of her and she stepped out as well. The object began to move toward the south, accelerating quickly, well above the forest crowns, headed out of sight.

We got back in the car and I sped back to the bridge which afforded a wide view of the night sky.

Nothing. Not one intensely bright object in the sky.

"Here's what we ought to do," I suggested. "Let's go home and each draw and write down what we saw before we talk."

We were both pretty adept illustrators, and being in the building trades as well as having done considerable forestry work, we were pretty good at estimating dimensions. We independently drew a cigar-shaped object, agreed on the color, and guessed the length at 70 (mine) to 80 (hers) feet.

It was clearly nothing either of us had ever seen before. (Or since, I might add.)

Later, oddly enough, I read the book *Incident at Exeter: Unidentified Flying Objects Over America Now,*[195] by John G. Fuller. Oddly because it wasn't the sort of book that usually drew me in.

This is the highly unlikely story of a putative abduction of a couple, purportedly taken up in a flying saucer by aliens who were supposedly interested in studying human biology in somewhat invasive ways.[196] I really don't remember much about the book ... except this: Our landlady was interviewed and quoted to the effect that she had seen a strange silent object descend over

195 G.P. Putnam's Sons, 1966

196 Sexually, if memory serves. Though that's true of many "abductions." Kate McKinnon's abduction stories on SNL® are to die for.

a power line and extend some kind of rod that connected to the line.

She was a very sane and sober sort.

On the other hand, she kept ducks. So think what you will.

The ducks could provide some sort of key.

Or not.

Lamentably I've lost track of our drawings over the ensuing decades. I'm quite certain I stuck them in my copy of R. Buckminster Fuller's *Synergetics: Explorations in the Geometry of Thinking* (Macmillan, 1975)[197], but I don't know where that copy landed. Maybe it was abducted?

Bucky would certainly have loved modern computer tech had he lived a few more decades! He was about as exotically nerdy as a body can be, and I'm the first to admit that while *Synergetics* made good sense, IMHO, *Synergetics 2: Further Explorations in the Geometry of Thinking* (Macmillan, 1979) left me entirely baffled. But that just now has me thinking: "Maybe I should take another stab at it. I might have a different cognitive platform after all these hazy crazy years."

Meanwhile modern computing brings us back to our story. Hara. Remember Hara? Seeker of rare birds? Hara became fascinated with the whole idea of surviving thylacines. She followed stories online, blowing up fuzzy pictures to see if she could make out what others saw in them. Was that a striped back or a series of moon shadows cast by nearby underbrush? What about that foot? Was the ankle shorter than a dog's?

She laughed knowingly at the Photoshopped® attempt by a young Mexican fraudster, seeing right away that the rear portion of the creature matched, line-for-line, stripe-for-stripe, a photo taken about a century ago. The reason that particular Tasmanian tiger's head was "accidentally" blocked from view in the fake was that in the original it was holding a chicken in its mouth. A dead giveaway to the thacyline-versed per the scam.

But *then* our protagonist, for that is what she has come to be, was taken in. "*Oh non! Quelque chose s'est mal passé!*"[198]

Someone supposedly residing in Tasmania had posted a YouTube® depicting a pair of thacylines seen in the medium distance, slightly blurred but definitely the creatures in question.

---

197 The sort of book that did draw me in.

198 I know that inserting an entire sentence in French will stretch you out a bit, but I think it's high time. What do you think this means? See page 119* for the exciting answer!

There was no mistaking them. Another brief scene included three pups, or, hmm, maybe they are "joeys," being marsupial. (?)

Here, finally, was proof-positive in a date-stamped video!

The supposed charitable organization involved sounded reputable, and they were dedicated to the preservation of this most terribly endangered species! Of course, they needed donations to continue their work.

Having hungered after oddballs and queer ducks and the elusive and phantasmal "cryptid" all her life, Hara was *thrilled!* Here was her chance to help out with the real deal!

She logged on to the organization's website and donated $500! I'll say this for her. "At least she wasn't risking life and limb." But ...

... computer generated graphics have come a long, long way. Why, just last week, a "deep fake" series purporting to be Tom Cruise®—practicing his golf swing, doing a magic trick and laughing at his own pratfall—went viral on TikTok®. Face it, if a talented geek can create a pretty convincing human performing unusual things, voice and all, it has to be more than simple to do the same with a slightly out-of-focus representation of a quick-moving critter.

Which it proved to be.

Sigh.

Hara is, understandably, crestfallen.

*"Oh no! Something went wrong!" As previously indicated, I've been reading Thomas Wolfe of late, and if there's one thing in his writing that drives me absolutely nuts it's when he goes on for whole paragraphs i*n la langue françai*s. That is, IMHO, expecting just *un peu trop* from your *lecteur moyen*,[199] whereas my habitual insertion of *un mot ou deux* is likely to "spice things up a bit" without obscuring the underlying *récit*. Therefore I have here quickly provided a translation of the phrase for the benefit of my non-Francophone readers.

Score: Bothwell #1, Wolfe #0.[200]

Oh, this note added later *in re*[201] the slaughter mentioned on page 114: This morning's (3/29/21) NYT® reports that Montana is about to open up the flood gates on wolf extermination again. Yes, a GOP governor and legislature. Love them some guns they do.

199 Honestly, it feels like posturing or "putting on airs."

200 Just sayin'.

201 Latin!

At a Loss

Consideration of Cook & Co.® (pages 113-114) coupled with musings regarding *Nice Noblets*® (page 102), inevitably encouraged my wandering mind into Bruce Chatwin's, *The Songlines*[202]. Didn't they you, into yours? Rather, his? Of course they did! And collaterally therefrom to Charles Mann, right? Though in a contextually semi-disparate manner, given that Mann wrote *1491: New Revelations of the Americas before Columbus* (Knopf, 2005) and didn't die outside of Nice, France. In fact, as of this morning, he hasn't died, offering a further contextual difference.

Chatwin "made up" the parts of his book that weren't true, a practice obviously dear to my heart. But the parts that were true? Icing on the literary cake IMHO. Butter on the fictional bread. Pearls in the pigsty even.

Well, maybe not that.

Avocado on the toast?

Speaking of losses, we lost a good one with Chatwin, much too early. Only 47 when he reached his date of expiry outside Nice. But as they say, "Only the young die good."

I was discussing this with Terry Sommers just this morning. You surely remember Terry.

No?

The woman we met way back on page 15, expressing her dismay—verging on deep miffededness—that the purportedly "organic" chestnuts she had purchased from Frankie the street vendor were, in fact, not.

It struck me just now that your failure to remember her is likely due to the one-dimensional picture painted during that bit of *contretemps*.[203] All you really learned about her was that she eats an organic diet and stands up for truth in advertising. Oh, and that at some point in her life she displayed a fondness for

---

202 A deep dive into Aboriginal culture that Chatwin regarded as a "novel" despite the historicity of his research and explication thereof (Penguin, 1987).

203 Note how saying the exact same word in French makes the situation seem somewhat more, shall we say, lurid? *Plus mystérieuse?*

Dove Bars®. That describes so many "good eggs" among your circle of friends that it doesn't offer much specificity. I get it.

"What else ought we to know?"

Good question.

Well, like so many of the "good eggs" that inhabit our vivid imaginations—mine anyway—she herds sheep![204]

In fact, that's how I happened to meet her in the first place. You see, I had a dental appointment and was running a little late, though, obviously, we all know that even if I'd raced like mad and landed in the waiting room at the strike of ten, I'd have had to twiddle for twenty minutes. [As I've observed, likely more than once in the course of my maundering, that's why they call it a waiting room and why they call us patients. They expect us to be.] As I rounded that curve over the last hummock before the straight away headed toward Fairview,[205] what should greet me but a flock of sheep! In the road.

This was/is not a good thing.

I pulled off in a driveway and got out to deal with the dire situation.

Now, if you've never wrangled a herd of sheep you've missed a very singular experience. Yeah, yeah, we've all herded cats, but cats are a piece of cake compared to a bahhh-ing bunch of woolly wanderers. I kind of got the mob headed off the road and up a gravel drive next to the pasture whence they'd clearly escaped, but one or another kept scooting around behind me, and once a few had altered course the rest would decide that was the deal. "Oh, we're going *that* way? Well, why not?"

Round and round we went. Fortunately the S-curve in the road caused drivers to slow, and the few cars that passed managed to miss the miscreants who returned to the pavement. I was exhausted, what with running and yelling, by the time Terry came down from the house with her Sheltie, Bosco. [She'd heard my shouting.]

Bosco was clearly well-trained and soon, with Terry's expert guidance and my amateur muddling, the flock was up the drive and in through the open gate.

She offered profuse thanks and also coffee and a slice of organic pecan pie, but I demurred, indicating that I was actually in kind of a rush headed for dental hell. [Yes, a root canal.]

---

204 This part is absolutely true, both dental appointment and sheep. Name changed however as part of my witness protection program.

205 I was living in Broad River township at the time. Also true.

"Well, how about you stop by on your way home? I can offer you lunch."

Something clicked for me. Maybe her dimples? As we've seen in dozens of short stories over several years, I'm kind of a sucker for dimples. I accepted. Numb or not.

Given that it's irrelevant to the current narrative, and wanting to protect the innocent, I'm disinclined to offer what ensued. Let's just say "We became very, very, very well acquainted over the subsequent months." *Intimement* doesn't do it justice.[206]

But that was some years ago and the fire burned low. We're still good friends, which is about as pleasant an outcome one might hope for in a former love affair. I've known worse.

So we were on the phone the other day, just after she'd read a draft[207] of the first story mentioned in the first sentence of the current *fabrication,* and she said, "Boy, oh boy, that sure reminds me of Australia!"

"What?" I hear you thinking. "She was in Australia?"

Indeed she was!

In college, back in the '80s, Terry met Steven Goolsby, an Aussie, and was smit. They were both seniors at the time and after graduation their parting was going to be one of those sweet sorrow things you read about in Shakespeare and so forth. Though they weren't "marrying types" they were pretty thoroughly "itemized" at that point and Steven said, "Sheila,[208] why'n't ya come along with me? We'd make a jolly time of it. What say?"[209]

Terry loves an adventure as much as any of us and she quickly agreed. They had a great few years until, as so often seems to happen to my characters, their roads diverged in a yellow wood. He'd decided to delve into Aboriginal culture and headed out on walkabout with an indigine he'd befriended. She found work on a sheep station in Queensland and fell in love with the fuzzy critters. A year or so later she had learned a good deal about sheep keeping and was feeling the tug of home.

Meanwhile, as the luck of the narrative would have it, her widowed grandmother had died, leaving the farm outside of

---

206 We're back to fiction here. Wishful thinking perhaps.

207 I always let my made-up characters proofread anything that might involve them. For accuracy's sake. Getting things straight from the virtual horse's mouth, so to speak.

208 Aussie slang. He's not confused about her name.

209 Sort of faking it here. But it's approximately how he framed it.

Fairview to Terry's folks, and, gosh! In this paragraph we discover that she is an only child! How fortuitous!

You can see right off where this leads.

A goodbye kiss blown at Steven, wherever the hell he was, and a one-way ticket home. The farm was free and clear of debt, having been in the family for generations, and Terry's parents were more than happy for her to assume the helm. For a good stretch she worked at Hickory Nut Gap® farm over in the next valley while slowly growing her flock. The rest is what's come to be known as "herstory."

Now that you've had a clearer glimpse of our "Sheila," we can get back to this morning's conversation.

"Your story about Banks and his confirmation bias rang so true for me."

"How's that?"

"Well, being from the South, I have to admit I was brought up with some pretty strong racist influences. It didn't really work for me, but I can't say I was immune, you know?"

"Hard to avoid. Stereotypes ..."

"Yeah. And fear of ..."

"The other?

"Right. And my time in Australia changed things ..."

"Otherness in another frame?"

"Yeah. Worked with a few Aboriginals, heard them called 'Abos,' which is a lot like 'Coon' in the states, a real slur. Or 'Nigger' for that matter. They call themselves "Blackfellas" but unless you're a friend they don't much like whites using the term. I worked side by side with two of them and they were wonderful friends to me. I didn't buy the reasons for racism there and it made me think hard about the biases I'd been imbued with back here."

"I've wondered about the word Abo ever since that song was popular. What was it, 'Tie Me Kangaroo Down, Sport'?"[210] Something about 'Let me Abos go loose, Lou, let me Abos go loose.' But I'm sorry to admit that I've been incurious enough never to follow up on it until just now."[211]

[Author pauses to DuckDuck® slavery in Australia.]

---

210 Rolf Harris's hit song from 1957. Don't think it would fly today, though the concluding verse remains quite amusing. "Tan me 'ide when Oi'm dead, Fred. Tan me 'ide when Oi'm dead. So we tanned 'is 'ide when 'e died, Clyde, and that's it 'angin ' on the shed."

211 7:18 a.m., 15 March 2021. The Ides. I should have expected something.

“Oh my! Not only was slavery a 'thing' in Australia starting with the first British settlement in 1788, but it has continued to the present! It wasn't even conclusively banned until 2018, if the Wikipedia® entry is accurate! (Though to be fair, banning of slavery was in the charter of the New South Wales colony at the time of its inception.)”

“Yeah. I heard about it during the time I was there. It was considered illegal, but out in the Outback, it wasn't always enforced. That was part of my awakening too. I came back a whole lot better informed.”

“Guess it was easier to self-examine when you were out of the old normal.”

“That's it. That's exactly it.”

[This space left blank both because I ran out of story, and also to give my readers the opportunity to reflect on the history of slavery in Australia. As of 2016 there were an estimated 16,000 people living under conditions of “modern slavery” on the continent, according to the Global Slavery Index. Here, stateside, of course, we don't condone slavery any longer. We just throw lots of Black people in prison and pay them pennies per hour to sew military uniforms, work in call centers and so forth.

Which, I've got to say, leaves me at a loss.]

Throwing in the Towel

I just got a text from one of you—who asked not to be named—asking about Melissa Tyner. Y'know, another one of the jurors you met on page 34? Trust me, I hadn't intended to walk out of this *mélange* without getting back to her, and now's as good a time as any.[212] So Ms. Anonymous? Thanks for the nudge!

Melissa is a case in point, just like Leonora Jensen[213] in that regard, though she isn't at all like Leonora in other ways. For one thing, and this looms large in my view, Melissa *doesn't* grow mushrooms in coffee grounds.

She's a tea drinker, which explains a lot, including the true fact that there's nary a bean nor a ground in her home![214]

By this time you have your author pretty well trained, so you don't even have to pepper me with questions like "What does she do?" I'll move right into that now.

The question itself is interesting, of course. Generally speaking, when we ask, "What does she/he do?" we are inquiring concerning a person's work life or profession, which, on closer examination is a bit odd. People do a lot of things other than work or profess.

Take Melissa for example. See?

The idea I'm driving at here is that while we learned that Leonora grows shiitake and oyster mushrooms that she then vends at the local tailgate market and, thinking back, that she patronizes Mike's Mechanical®, that she lives with a chicken chef named Mel who has a "thing" about Baby Yoda®, and that, in clement weather, she's not above hitching a ride now and again—a few fairly sketchy details—we didn't actually learn much about what she "does."

Here's a short list: reads science fiction, bakes pasties, pets her cats, does laundry (alternating with Mel) ... and, get this —she always *hangs* laundry to dry![215] She and Mel don't even own

212 7:25 a.m. EDT, 16 March 2021 to be precise.

213 See page 77.

214 *Rara avis,* indeed!

215 Reminding us of Eleanor, the particle physicist in "Clothesline," *Waist Not, Want Knot,* Brave Ulysses Books, 2020, who BTW "professes."

a dryer! Green as can be. Let's see: she's a film buff, particularly keen on the '40s and '50s; likes to skinny dip in remote creeks; was on her high school track team; does crosswords (woman after my own heart, there), always eats sushi with chopsticks; calls her Mom every Sunday; went to an "escape room" once and hated it, um ...cleans the cats' litter box daily ...um ... well, maybe that's enough for just now.

But you see my point, don't you?

Of course you do.

I bet next time someone asks you "What does she/he do?" or even, "What do *you* do?" you'll have fun,fun,fun answering.

"She brushes her teeth three times a day!"

"Remember that 'step on a crack' thing from when you were a kid? He *never* steps on a crack! To this day."

"I think about life on Mars!"

See how much more giggly that can be instead of "She's a nurse. He's a shoe salesman. I'm a short story writer." [Bor-ing!]

So, let's think hard now. (I mean, *you've* already been thinking about Melissa, but *I've* been busy writing this whole time.) What does Melissa do?

Ah. Got it. Sad to report—and I hope this doesn't make you think less of her—she obsesses. There's one in every crowd, and more than likely on every jury. But, here's the thing. She obsesses about ... um ... oh, right ... *folding laundry!* (Italics hers. She is just *that* intense about it.)

Now, being a good egg like most of my protagonists, she, like Leonora and Mel, doesn't own a dryer, using a clothesline for that purpose. On the other hand, given her OCD—to put a label on it[216]—*she irons her sheets!* And pillowcases, of course, not to mention her blouses, skirts, vests, slacks *and* blue jeans! Blue jeans! Obviously the electricity used to warm the iron carves a bit into her carbon-control line-drying effort, and if you see her you might contribute to my attempt to get her to obsess about the climate just a little more.

Fortunately she draws the line at panties and socks, though she does fold them very, very neatly, and gosh, if you'd look in her drawers [in the dresser ... what were you thinking?] the way she lines things up is astonishing! Neat rows of folded attire, arranged by color using ROYGBIV as her organizational template. Same thing with the closet, hangers evenly spaced.

Also fortunately, she's never looked in my drawers or in

216 Mildly, not morbidly so. We want this to be amusing. Not making fun.

my clothes or linen closets. I suspect if she found out I never fold a fitted sheet, a pair of undies, a handkerchief ... she'd tear up her contract and refuse to be part of the current volume.

I'm inclined to believe that Melissa's *inclination,* to put a bit more positive spin on it—that is to say her "type of inclination,"—is part of the glue that holds the world together. I'm pretty sure I'm a little on the other side of average from Lissa, and there are others (not naming any names here, but you know some, I feel sure) who are *way* on the other end of that spectrum. If it weren't for people like her I have a strong feeling that we would end up missing a lot more than, say, a sock or two in the laundry. Instead of *finally* finding things in the last place we looked,[217]—car keys, glasses, cellphones, kids at the mall, etc.—we probably wouldn't even be able find the "place."

None of the preceding bears directly on the subject of today's lesson. As was noted regarding the particle physicist[218] or cosmologist who invented a home-grown clothes pole:

> "That was an interregnal thought, the sort of thing we each deal with day after day, between the buttons, as the saying goes, of the important work of our lives.
>
> "It often seems to border on the miraculous that we get anything done at all, what with our inventive minds, opposable thumbs and inclination to get into mischief."[219]

Isn't that the truth?!

Having escaped that *interrègne,* we can move right along.

Back before the time of cholera people were given to gathering in public places to eat, drink, be entertained, gossip, laugh to the point of tears and so forth. Really, they did. Seems a long time gone just now, like a half-remembered dream.[220]

But it was real, and Lissa was hanging with her crowd at Jack of the Wood® in downtown Asheville one Friday evening when a *very* neatly dressed stranger tentatively approached her.

"Hi."

"Oh, hi."

---

217 I know I'm easily amused, but that phrase always tickles me, contemplating those who continue to look after they find things, though to be fair, that sort of describes a good scientist.

218 See footnote 208 in *Seize You on the Dark Side of the Moo.*

219 *Waist Not, Want Knot,* p. 160.

220 7:44 a.m. EDT, 17 March 2021

"My name is Ryan, and I couldn't help but notice that it appears on careful consideration that you must *iron your jeans!*"

This is not exactly what most of us would think of as a smooth pickup line. Lissa was a bit taken aback. Was this Ryan person criticizing her? She cocked her head and put on a serious face. "In fact, *Ry-an* (underlined italics hers), *I do*. Do you have a problem with that?" Thus setting herself up for a definitive brush off.

"Oh, no! I think that is so-o coo-ool! I mean they're obviously well worn with the slightly faded areas at the knees and some minor fraying just visible at the cuffs, but they're clearly starched and ironed and they look so damn good on you! I just had to cross the room to inform you regarding my observation. It isn't the sort of analysis one should keep to oneself." He nodded his head and added, "You made my day. Seeya." With which he waved the beer mug in his hand, nodded, and turned to go.

So, wow, she thought. That was amazing! He hadn't been hitting on her! He appreciated her thoughtful attention to her attire. He was obviously sincere. She followed him across the barroom to where he was rejoining some friends at one of the high-top tables you likely recall. She reached out and tapped his shoulder.

"Ryan, my name's Melissa, but my friends call me Lis,[221] and I just wanted to tell you that [pause, then with emphasis] *that* was probably the nicest compliment I've ever had the pleasure to receive. Thank you so very much!"

Having already exceeded any previous level of "forward" in her repertoire, she added another "Thanks!" with a quick nod and returned to her slot at the bar before he could reply.

"Lis, What was that all about?" queried Eleanor[222].

"Oh, nothing much." (We see her "downplaying" here.)

"It was *something*. I've never seen you do *that* before."

"I just got the nicest compliment is all."

Before Eleanor could continue her inquisition, Ryan had returned to Lissa's side. "It wasn't meant as a compliment," he

221 You note right away here that the hypocoristic I've been using makes it clear that while I have Melissa under contract for her appearance in this book, we obviously aren't "friends" in any meaningful measure.

222 One and the same. Eleanor, we remember, teaches at UNC Asheville, making friendship with Melissa entirely plausible, thus saving us the mental anguish of inventing and remembering the name of a new character in this era of late-stage capitalism. Need proof? Note "Lis."

intoned. "I mean if it seemed like I had intended it as a compliment you might think I was angling for something. It was simply the truth as I deduced it, accurately as it happens, to be."

"That makes it even better. Ryan, this is my best friend, Ellie Rigby. Ellie, my new favorite acquaintance, Ryan."

They did the "nice to meet you stuff" but we can skip that.

Ryan, it turned out, shares Lissa's "inclination" though he manifests it in somewhat different ways. Over the next hour or so, sitting in the front booth (whose occupants had cleared out, as had Eleanor who knows a "two's company" moment when she sees one, being a particle physicist, a cosmologist and all), he admitted that while he always took care to dress neatly ...

"I noticed. It's nice."

... he'd never thought of *pressing* his jeans,[223] but it was on his personal bucket list as of tonight. He was already planning his Saturday itinerary. "I'm going to get up at my usual time, 7 a.m., make a cup of tea, feed the cat, prepare some granola with oat milk, take my vitamins ... do you take yours in the same order every day?"

(She nods, fascinated.)

"Shower and shave, brush my teeth, comb my hair, then select a shirt and trousers and hang them on the valet stand ..."

"Oh, I have one too!"

"... select matching T-shirt, briefs and socks, then dress and select white or black running shoes depending on the day's motif. Then I plan to go online to check ratings with Consumer Reports® and possibly CNN®, then look in on various retail outlets regarding purchase of an ironing board and iron, and having determined the best price on the best quality item, weighing the two in consideration of affordability, I will make note of the destination on my cellphone and then, depending on the store opening hours, I will either proceed to that address or if, say, they don't open until 10 a.m., I will reorganize my pencil drawer and, if time allows, my string drawer as well. Do you sort by length?"

Well, well. You can imagine Lissa getting a little googley-eyed by this point. She nods and almost whispers, "Oh, yes. String

223 His non-denim trousers and shirts are all Sta-Prest® of course, and he does use a dryer (we'll get him with the program eventually). As I observed in one or another book in recent years, the advent of wrinkle-free garments has been credited with a diminution in male inclination to marry since the early 1960s. Wives having been previously so tasked.

and pencils!"

"Pencils by color?"

"No. All of mine are the same 6B KOH-I-NOOR TOISON D'OR®, you know the ones with the white stripe near the top?"

"Damn. I never thought of that one-color bit, but that means you must do ..."

"Crosswords? Yep."

"And do you have a KOH-I-NOOR rubber eraser too?"

"Three. For back-up."

Well, I think you probably think you know where this is headed. Exchange of phone numbers and what all.

Which it did, that evening in the first week of March, 2020. Oh, and before they parted she reminded him to pick up a can of spray starch.

But now I'm inclined to think you probably have had to have a further think or two. How does that calendric date figure in?

Oh, they texted and talked[224] and set up a date for Saturday, the 13th, and both were looking *way* forward to it. Ryan, for one thing, really wanted to show off his starched, pressed jeans. But then the news broke wide open regarding the looming pandemic.

For most of us "thinkers," that dictated being pretty darn careful, wearing a mask when in public, avoiding indoor crowds ... you know the drill. But for Ryan and Lissa,[225] sharing their—being kind here—"inclination," dating was an instant no-go. Period.

They both triple-mask. At home. Alone.

I guess they are what you'd have to call "metro-textuals" at this point, but as for intimate personal interactions? Pending their vaccinations, they've just thrown in the towel.[226]

---

224 He informed her that CNN® ranked the Maytag® M400 No.1.

225 Incidentally, and no surprise, Lissa is the modern equivalent of a file clerk, though digital rather than paper-based. She is *good!* And she was working remotely long before the current time of cholera. Office environments are a little too disorderly for her keen sensibility.

226 By the by, this profound consideration of the concept of when and what and "with what" to iron has trotted me back to my young years in the 1950s when my family had a "mangle" in the basement laundry room. For those who've never seen that word used anywhere other than in relation to an automobile wreck, a war zone, or "farm machinery eating people's arms and legs" as described in John Prine's "Ain't hurtin' nobody," (*Lost Dogs and Mixed Blessings,* 1995), a mangle is an ironing

Lâcher prise[227]

At this point we've revisited most of the principal players in the infamously ignoble *Noblet*® trial except for the accused/convicted/exonerated Greta Strenberg and her formerly alleged accomplice, Geoffrey Merced. Oh, and Alice Jensen and Larry Morris, the witnesses.

So what's the deal?

Greta, we know, is a clarinet player of long standing employed as a legal secretary by Greenberg, Thompson, Lutz, Hunter & Phillips, LLC.[228] Geoff we recall "works online for a software company in Nevada, and his legal address is out west. He's about as low-profile as a person can get. His life is encrypted and block-chained out the yin-yang."

As for Jensen and Morris, the evidentiary trail is pretty slim. They attended a party at that scurrilous scoundrel Cappy Thornsen's place and witnessed a brouhaha. A tumultuous one.

Probably the fact that all four of these folks attended that fateful get-together should give us pause.

---

device with a four-foot-wide rotating, tubular, padded, cloth-covered ironing surface and a heated, curved bar that's depressed with a knee lever. You feed flats—mostly sheets, pillowcases, tablecloths and napkins—onto the roller and lower the bar. Often you'd use a spray bottle to moisten. The mangle draws in the cloth and drops it underneath, perfectly pressed—as long as you don't leave an inadvertent fold in the inserted object, in which case you end up with a perfectly pressed wrinkle. (Obviously sheets are creased due to their dimensions.) I only mention it here because it was one of my chores from about 8-12 years of age. Then we moved and it was left behind. The point being that I have *standing* as well as *seating* when it comes to discussion of *pressing business.* [I do so hate it when footnotes run over into a succeeding story, but there are times when it absolutely cannot be avoided.]

227 Yes, this is "letting go," but as previously noted I've already used that title upslope (page 73), and given that this phrase is absolutely *à propos vis à vis* the present parable, this translation permits its use without causing undue confusion for Book Club participants.

228 We've gotten to know Del Hunter from this crowd. The others didn't actually "participate."

...
...
...

I hope that was long enough. But you do really get to wondering, don't you? Do you know anyone else who was there?

Think hard.

Neither do I. Our close friends, I'm pretty certain, have a bit better judgment. Y'know what I'm sayin'? [*in re* more anon.]

Anyway, an interesting thing you probably don't know yet is that Greta and Larry used to be an item, and—get ready for it!—so were Alice and Geoff! Small world!

!!

As it happens Alice and Geoff were part of the Nevadan diaspora, refugees fleeing the West as summer temperatures began to hit triple digits with uncomfortable frequency. Not long after they moved here Alice met Greta at a laundromat and they clicked. Soon enough the two couples were socializing and so forth, and they drew close. Quite, quite close. Very, very quite. Close as in, well, how can I put this delicately in case young ears are hearing you "sub-vocalize" just now. [Don't be embarrassed, a lot of readers do that.] Oh, I've got it! A film reference that tender ears are much too young to recall.

They went all "Bob and Carol and Ted and Alice"—which is their business, and who are we to judge? But while that sort of *affaire à quatre* might occasionally work out, it's more often the case, IMHO, that ... hmmm, I suppose Ellie Rigby could tell you definitively, but it's likely better if I paraphrase since she tends to drift off into long strings of mathematical equations.

What Ellie might suggest: "The short of it is that shoving all that hot matter together is more likely to cause fission than fusion."[229] After the explosion the couplets were rearranged and somewhat estranged, actually disarranged, until their several selves' sensibilities led to an exchange—mostly texts—and the former friends fashioned a phase change. [This is getting too silly. If I keep this up I'll end up typing "~~driving range~~"—dammit—and now have to quickly remind you that golf is not a sport. So we'll just put a line through that. Feeling better already.]

This is an area where a particle physicist knows whereof she speaks. Ellie, by the way, has a fun sense of humor and when she's away from her office she hangs a sign on her door done up in

229 Some energetic motion was surely involved.

Magic Marker®, an idea she sometimes says she borrowed from Robert Oppenheimer, one of those fathers of the atomic bomb, maybe even *the* father[230] —no telling if he did the hanky-panky.

Anyway when the dust settled they realized, heck, they'd been friends before, right? And wasn't this simpler?

Yes it was.

One thing the foursome had discovered during their time "very close together" was the amazing comfort of Egyptian cotton sheets, and they all agreed the luxury was worth the price.

Which brings us, at last, to the story part of this story.

[I was getting concerned that we'd never climb the hill.]

Here's something you almost certainly *didn't* guess about Alice: she's really keen on ancient Egypt. Really, really keen. In fact a conversation I had with her led to my suggestion back on page 50 regarding storage of nuclear waste. You see? There is a coherent thread running through here after all, and more than likely it's a thread of Egyptian cotton, which, due to growing conditions in that storied land, has exceptionally long fibers.

In any event, from the time she was a wee wad Alice[231] loved Egyptian picture books, and as she matured took to reading everything she could get her hands on regarding those magical days of hieroglyph and mummification and trepanning and clay jars full of excised organs. [Except the brain. That, they drained.]

She was really in her glory in 2010 when the road show, *Tutankhamun: The Golden King and the Great Pharaohs®* landed in Denver. She and Geoff drove almost 14 hours from

---

230 I made this up. But he *might* have had such a sign, right?

231 Another thread entirely, but do note that Alice is the name of a town almost dead center in Australia: e.g. "Alice Springs," which is amusing in its way since the Todd River, which flows through town, is dry 95% of the time. The point being that this connects the name of our current "person of interest" to stories on pages 113 and 118, disproving your theory that I simply bump around like a pinball.

Spring Valley[232] and spent two days exploring the exhibit. Alice really couldn't get her fill of statuary and relics.

They were a little disappointed that old Tut couldn't make the show, the Egyptian government having decided, following his *The Treasures of Tutankhamun®* (1972–1981) World Tour that both the mummy and the iconic golden burial mask were too fragile to make another appearance. But it was nice to know that he hadn't been ground up for use as a supplement.

No, really. As I mentioned in *Whale Falls: An exploration of belief and its consequences:*[233]

> [In the 1880s] "Egyptologists drew overflow crowds to lectures which culminated in unwrapping a cadaver. With scissors and knives, sometimes with chisels and saws (old resins can be stout), and always with dramatic flourish, the experts would reveal the windings, the amulets, the jewelry and finally the naked torso of a 3,000-year-old decedent.

Then, many were ground up and peddled as life-lengthening nostrums. "Look how well *they* were preserved!"

Honest. You can't make this stuff up.

People being people—by the by—during the unwrapping events? Exposure of the genitals was always a crowd pleaser. *"Sic vitium unquam ad,"*[234] as they said in olden days.

But we're wandering a bit, so back on track.

One of the most fascinating and unexpected items Alice noted was an archaic Egyptian pillow.

"Ah," I hear you thinking, "Now we're back to Egyptian cotton!"

Nope. We're back to Egyptian sandstone![235]

"What?!" I hear you thinking.

I'll let Alice tell you about that.

Alice?

"Oh, hi there folks! Ancient Egyptian pillows were sort of scoop shaped wooden, alabaster, glass or stone headrests, which doesn't probably seem very comfortable. I mean, can you imagine? Your head kind of stuck, and you sure wouldn't want to put your cheek on a rock. But actually they were only used for the

---

232 Another bit of wishful thinking I'm afraid. Like Alice Springs, Spring Valley, Nevada, is in the middle of a desert.

233 Brave Ulysses Books, 2010. Page 128.

234 Latin!!

235 See page 21 and footnote 23.

dead, who tend to not roll around a whole lot, particularly after they were wrapped in resin-soaked Egyptian cotton[236] sheets, and the idea seemed to involve making the departed more comfortable. Pillows and sheets! Nice thought."

[Point of clarification: We note here that while Alice is "talking about pillows" it isn't probably what we usually refer to as "pillow talk," which she engaged in with Geoff and now Larry.]

Alice, why don't you tell them about the brains too? We mentioned that on the previous page.

"Um, well, for ancient Egyptians the head of a human was considered to be the essence of life and sacred—presumably because cutting it off sort of reduced social interaction—and keeping the corpse's head raised was believed to prevent demons from getting inside, being as it was now hollow. On the flip side, they believed thinking occurred in the heart and that the brain didn't have any important function. So while they saved all of the internals in amphorae—though that's a Greek word (αμφορέας[237]) not Egyptian

أمفورا

which is not actually "Egyptian," being Arabic[238]—to ensure that the important parts would be available in the afterlife, fact is, they tossed the old noodle before they bundled the body.

"And if you think about that, why exactly do you think you think with your head? I mean, we know, at least those of us who "think," think that we think with our heads, but why do we think that? Is it because we think of ourselves as being behind our eyes, looking out? Or between our ears? It really isn't at all obvious. If you were raised by wolves, for example, would you come up with that on your own?"

See folks? Alice is deep. Way deep.

"I'm not finished."

Oh, OK.

"For instance if you use an online program you may think the thinking is going on in your computer when in fact it's going on at a data farm in Charlotte or Jakarta or who knows where."

See? She thinks about thinking just like ... "

---

236 "Aha!" You say. "We *are* back to Egyptian cotton!" I concede the point. But this is factually moot. My recent reading suggests they used linen.

237 Greek!!

238 Arabic! Spoken in Egypt, but not "Egyptian" *per se.* ←*Latin!*

"Look. I'm not finished. OK?"

Fine with me. Be that way.

"The other interesting thing I wanted to tell you, if this Bothwell person would quit interrupting, is what Bruce Chatwin mentioned on page 271 of the Penguin paperback edition of *The Songlines,* and I quote:

> "The ancient Egyptians believed the seat of the soul was in the tongue: the tongue was a rudder or steering-oar with which a man steered his course through the world."

Are you finished?

[Alice smiles and nods. I tell you this because, obviously, you can't see her just now.]

As I was saying, Alice thinks about thinking, like Ellie. Ellie is deep too, as are most particle physicists, and this is the thing I've been aiming at for more than four pages now.

"And tongues and brains and clay pots full of innards."

Thanks Alice. I'm [pause] *moving along* now.

Eleanor, now that we're considering her in a more serious light, puzzles with mathematics at the leading edge of physics. She's very much in the same ballpark as William Bryce, who we recall as a member of the jury in the *Noblet®* trial and as the generous husband who graced his wife with a Klein bottle. [It will come as no surprise that they actually work together at the university. Particle physics is not a major job category in a small city.]

[There are but two and these are they.]

Oh, you should hear the banter by the water cooler! She'll quip:

$$G_{\mu\nu} + \Lambda g_{\mu\nu} = \frac{8\pi G}{c^4} T_{\mu\nu}$$

And he'll come back with something like:

$$d_p = \int_0^{t_0} \frac{c}{a(t)}\, dt.$$

Then they'll laugh and laugh, only calming down a little when one or the other takes it a step further. "I don't think we've completely resolved whether Hawking was correct regarding the distinction between an actual event horizon and an apparent one. Does that bother you as much as it bothers me?"

"Well, from a practical perspective—an observational one

that is—doesn't it seem a distinction without a difference?"

"There's that."

And then, back to work.

But the thing is—as we all surely know—deep thinkers who are lost in the fog of quantum theory are sometimes baffled by the prosaic. Sure, give them action at a distance when protons and anti-protons go for a spin, or perhaps some fascinating new data point from the latest mash-up in the Large Hadron Collider® and they'll talk your ear off, but hand them simple household tasks?

Nothing. Crickets. Quiet as roadkill.[239]

Eleanor, for instance, has puzzled for years per the question "Would Drano® let you hurt your pipes?" She finally had to simply use it, flush it with hot water, and let it go.

On the flip side, listening to Thea Gilmore for example, Eleanor just nods her head. "Yep. Nails it. Language in the sky."

"3pm. Blue as a road sign,
With a gag and some cheap wine
Sun's in my eyes between
The smoke trails of aircraft,
The kite tails and light shafts
There's a language in the sky
There's a language in the sky
There's a language in the sky
There's a *language* in the sky"[240]

"And cats, and ibises, they would mummify anything ...
Alice. *Alice.* Listen, the story *est fini. Comprendre?*

239 I swiped this turn of phrase from songwriter Thea Gilmore's title song on the album *Avalanche,* Compass Records, 2004. A brilliant poet.

240 Ibid.

Giving In

Lawrence Edgerton Morris* has always felt just a little "special" because of his initials, and, honestly, I can't blame him. I bet you would too.

By day he's a bike mechanic, and a good one at that. He works for a shop downtown, a job that pays pretty well because the owner both values the quality of his workmanship and, frankly, doesn't want to lose him to the competition, though to be clear, Larry loves his job and likes his boss so he's not looking around.

His boss, Tim, we recall,[241] fell in love with Irma the landscaper soon after she brought her mountain bike in for a tuneup. Actually that (ongoing) love affair (years!) is one of the reasons Tim hired Larry. Tim had built up the business as a one-man show, but the burgeoning trade coupled with wanting to take a little more time off to spend with Sweet Pea suggested that he share the load.

[Havoc, by the way, is quite appreciative of having a second pair of hands to apply the therapeutic massage necessary to a sophisti-cat. We do remember that Tim could wax a little absent-minded when adjusting brakes, mulling life on other planets and the puzzle of whether this whole scenario we're engaged in is just an elaborate touchy-feely hologram.]

We also recall that Larry was itemized with Greta before the four-way *gambader,* then paired off with Alice. But surely he does other things besides tinkering with velocipedes and diddling.

I'm not going to play that trick again of just listing all the things he does. Gimmicks only work once IMHO. [Consider yourself spared.]

But there is one really, really interesting thing in which he engages. It is so highly unusual that I'm convinced that no one in your circle has ever gone there. I'm sure I don't know another soul who's so dabbled.

I'll give you a hint.

He found his first one under a pile of leaf mold!

---

241 "A Little Like a Link of Chain," on page 36 of the amazing collection, *Fifty Wheys to Love Your Liver,* Brave Ulysses Books, 2018

!!

It's about five inches long and has polka dots! Guesses?

That's right! He breeds salamanders!

Sure, sure, a lot of us *keep* salamanders as pets because they are ideal, particularly for, say an apartment dweller. They don't take up a lot of space, they don't bark all the time and annoy the neighbors, they don't claw the furniture and, get this—they can live for 20 or more years in captivity! This means your episodes of heartbreak come at wider intervals than with most dogs or cats, though Pomonella[242] made 22 or so.

She was a real sweetheart too.

Now, you noticed I said, "They don't take up a lot of space" in the previous paragraph, but that's if you, like most of us, only have three or four of the slippery little boogers around the house.[243]

Larry has about three dozen breeders[244] just now! Four species! Fourteen aquaria! Big ones! With live bog plants! And little ponds! And misting gizmos that keept the humidity just where his little folks like it.

He's breeding the spotted, the red, the long-tailed and the red-legged species! And he returns the offspring to the wild!

Now I've got your attention, I see. And you want to know what his breeders eat.

As you know, in the wild they eat worms and grubs and maggots and crickets and flies and centipedes and slugs and ... well, actually they're opportunistic and eat just about anything they can get in their mouths, including other salamanders if that yummy-tummy opportunity knocks. So of course, when they've laid eggs in the little pond down at the end of the aquarium, the grown-ups have to be moved into another habitat or they'd be very likely to eat the kids which reminds us of Jonathan Swift's most famous essay: *A Modest Proposal For preventing the Children of Poor People From being a Burthen to Their Parents or Country, and For making them Beneficial to the Publick.*

---

242 Originally named Tammy Faye because her facial coloration looked like badly applied makeup, Pomonella was a stray who sank her felines into my hand when I rescued her. This was a strategic move on Po's part, ensuring a quarantine period regarding rabies. Thence we bonded.

243 Also, the largest salamander in the world is the Chinese giant salamander. It can grow to be almost 6 feet in length and weigh 110 pounds. So "don't take up a lot of space" isn't invariably true.

244 And many, many more when batches of eggs hatch!

I think I can claim without fear of contradiction that I am handier with titles than Mr. Swift. But I will give him points for his ability to shock.

Viz: "A young healthy child well nursed, is, at a year old, a most delicious nourishing and wholesome food, whether stewed, roasted, baked, or boiled; and I make no doubt that it will equally serve in a *fricassée*[245] or a ragout."

We see here that Swift had a knack for irony. The first part of his essay set up the reader by discussing the sad state of affairs for the downtrodden, ill-clothed and ill-fed masses.

You can practically hear the upper-crusters muttering to themselves, "Another damn bleeding heart liberal!" Only to then hit the "unthinkable" proposal, after which to wonder where, exactly, the purportedly toothsome babies might be procured and at what price. "Are they truly both tasty and reasonably affordable?"

I'm not exactly clear what twelve months amounts to in salamander-years. Um. If they can live to be 20 and we live to be, say, 80, then I guess we divide by four, so we're talking three months. A three-month-old salamander would definitely be bite-size for the grownups.

The Smithsonian Conservation Biology Institute® states that the Appalachian region is home to more salamander species than anywhere else in the world, making it a hot spot for salamander biodiversity. Perhaps that's why so many locals keep them as pets. [Duly noted: Salamanders don't have ears, so naming them would be pointless. They are *not* going to come when called.]

But breeding them? That seems pretty specialized.

You may not have known that Larry is possessed of an M.S. degree in biology! Which, you'll now think, makes one wonder how he ended up doing bike repairs. That isn't an obviously smooth trajectory and whether uphill or down is debatable.

And you're right! It involved heartbreak. Poor man. It was hard for Deborah too, of course, but she's the one who saw the writing on the wall and understood it.

"នេះនឹងមិនដំណើរការក្នុងរយៈពេលវែងទេ[246]

---

245 And like your author he wasn't shy about using a little French to spice things up!

246 "This isn't going to work in the long run," for those of you who share Larry's lack of linguistic breadth.

[Larry, for his part, didn't and doesn't read Khmer.]

Nor is feeding the herd an easy task for Larry. In your own amphibian husbandry you've surely discovered that the pet section at the local supermarket is unlikely to stock maggots and slugs, or, at minimum, is unlikely to *admit* to it. My guess is you buy crickets at a local pet store and red wigglers from a local bait shop.

That's fine, as far as it goes. Your little slipperies will survive just fine on a limited diet. I'm not trying to make you feel guilty here. But ...

The thing is, if you want your slimy charges to make babies, you need to provide a wider range of nutrition. So Larry has a worm farm in a lidded storage container to which he adds leftovers from the kitchen. He has a tank full of guppies, and he's gone so far as to pick up road-killed squirrels or rabbits and set them out in the backyard to let flies generate maggots.[247] What's more, when he's digging in the garden he always keeps a container at hand for the grubs he unearths.

Then, too, he lets fruit flies infest rotten produce in order to generate tiny maggots for the youngsters. He is truly something else.

But I see a hand up.

"Pomonella?"

Ah, you're wondering why a cat named Tammy Faye ended up being called Pomonella.

Well, it's like this. I named her Tammy Faye because I thought that was hilarious. At the time Jim and Tammy Faye Bakker were embroiled in some kind of financial scandal, as is so frequently the case with rich and famous religious proselytizers. It's usually either money or unsavory/kinky/extramarital sex, and all too often all of the above.

But I soon came to understand that naming a cat for a TV shyster was unkind to the recipient, so I cast about for something more elevating. My sense of humor gave in to my sense of propriety.

I am not really a bad person.

---

247 Reminding us of the Body Farm® in Tennessee, discussed at fascinating length in "Jawboned," the 16th of 40 amazing stories in *Self-Evident: We Hold These Tooths,* Brave Ulysses Books, 2021. The Body Farm is a research center where expired people are scattered around in various circumstances to explore how the situation of a corpse plays out over time. Forensic science at its most ... whatever.

Po's coloration was truly scrambled—not just her facial "Tammy-esque" makeup. She looked like a dust rag had mated with a sort of half-breed Siamese that was the product of a pure bred and maybe a mud puppy[248] if that gives you some sense of it. I finally decided she looked moth-eaten and turned to *The Audubon Society Field Guide to North American Insects and Spiders.®*

There I learned that the specific name of the apple codling moth is *pomonella* and gosh, this is apple country!

That sounded kind of pretty.

QED.

"Crumbling"—continued from page 105

OK, we have half a page here to wind things up.

What Larry tells people about the eighth grade *contretemps*[334] is this, and let's bear in mind that at age 47 he's had many years to tidy up his memory. As I've mentioned in various other books, but I think not herein, careful research has shown that our clearest memories are those that suddenly come to mind after many years. The ones we revisit, we change: We forget things. We fill in the blanks. We make stories better. [Something I'm sure you've hoped I'd do at some point.]

Larry thought he was a really bright kid, holding himself in extremely high esteem. And, hey, he was a reader and did well on tests, which is how our late-stage capitalist society has decided to determine "is our children learning?"[335]

He'd gotten nearly straight A's on every report card and scored up in the high ninetieth percentile on those damn standardized end of grade tests. Right up to grade eight. Oh, he did fine on the reading portion, but some of the questions on the math test really stumped him. Imagine that child's crumbling self image!

---

334 French! One last "world language" before quitting time

335 President George W. Bush. Yes, he really said that.

---

248 *Necturus maculosis,* yes, a salamander! Not that cats and salamanders ever actually "bred" before the invention of CRISPR technology. The pet stores of the future are already in the works folks!

* LEM. As in Lunar Excursion Module. "One small step for a man," etc. And lest you think he's kind of "out there" attaching his initials to a space craft, that was his parents doing. The Morrises were quite keen on the moon landings and intentionally graced their first-born with that acronym. It's better than Franklin Franklin at least. (See page 13.)

Handing Off

One of Terry's fond memories of Australia is of a visit to The National Dinosaur Museum®[249] in Canberra and oddly enough, the fossil that most intrigued her was *not* that of a dinosaur! It was a *Procoptodon!*

Procoptodon goliah, in fact, almost nine feet tall!

You don't see one of them every day, now do you? (Though I'm sure they've figured in your less sanguine dreams.) And weighing in at something more than 500 pounds I expect you're glad of it! [Not the dreams, obviously.]

But now that we're Down Under again perhaps we should check in with Steven Goolsby, who lured Terry to his stomping grounds and later wandered off. As men will. As men will.

Doubtless you've been wondering just where he went and more than a few of you have suspected for 20 or so pages that he didn't, in fact, go "walkabout" in the Aboriginal sense of that term but rather "ran around" in the sense of womanizing.

It was both.

He did head off with a Blackfella named Donley-Don with whom he was close enough that he could comfortably use that term. While they hiked Donley-Don told Steven stories of the Lizard Ancestor—the ones, at least, that weren't tribal secrets—and how the Lizard Man came to die.

It's no wonder that Lizard Ancestor looms large in the Aboriginal psyche. When humans first arrived in Australia they were greeted by *Megalania,* which name might remind one of a recent U.S. First Lady, Or of her megalomaniac spouse], but *Meg* was not a similarly gracious hostess. Nay, nay. *Megalania* was a 23-foot-long relative of today's Komodo dragon. A couple of million years ago it was the largest lizard on earth.

But a week or so into the venture Steven managed to poke himself with a Phoenix palm acanthophyll and the tip of the spine

249 I'm making this up. Full disclosure: I've never been to Australia (though I've been to Oklahoma). But my guess is that if any museum in Australia has *Procoptodon* fossils—one must—it would be the The National Dinosaur Museum in Canberra® which is a real place. The thing is, if I were Terry I would definitely have seen to it that I visited that museum.

broke off in his thigh. Hurtin' for certain doesn't come close.

Soon the wound became infected, and while Donley-Don was quite good at foraging for food in the wilderness he wasn't up to snuff on wild medicinals. So they walked/limped to a small town with a clinic where a nurse practitioner[250] with a pleasant and professional bedside manner soon went a step further: i.e. she was no longer "beside" his bed three days into his convalescence.

Oh. He didn't resist, to be sure.

Resistance would have been futile in his weakened state and considerably less exciting. "Hey ninety-eight point six it's good to have you back again,"[251] he hummed. Be that as it may.

Boy. "Be that as it may" covers a whole lot of ground.

Consider, if you will, Osama the crocodile. Kind of right up there with the good ole *Procoptodon,* right?

Osama used to live in Lake Victoria and lunch on unwary villagers. It's believed that he consumed all or part of 83 unlucky folks before he was taken into custody—no easy trick with a sixteen foot long, one-ton reptile.

From 1991 forward the septuagenerian croc gobbled up a tenth of the villagers in Luganga, Uganda, not stopping at simply snarfing unwary swimmers. Oh, no! Osama would leap into boats to grab fishermen, dash up on shore to snatch women and girls, and in 2005, lunched on a 12-year-old boy. This proved to be his last free-range meal.

Wildlife officials with a team of fifty men baited and hooked the beast and towed him thrashing to shore where he was ... I know what you're thinking. "He was killed."

Nope. That's what wildlife officials in the United States do with renegade alligators, but Ugandans are more practical. Osama was sold to Uganda Crocs, LTD®, purveyors of fine crocodile-skin handbags to the fashion conscious in Italy and Korea.

"So he *was* killed after all?"

Nope. It seems that a 75-year-old crocodile is in his sexual prime. So now old Osama diddles[252] the girls and doesn't have to devote his days to stalking prey. Whether he would rather enjoy a

250 We'll come up with a name later. And, yes, she'd been lonely too long.

251 "Her lovin' is the medicine that saved me ..." etc. from "98.6" from the Keith album *98.6,* Mercury Records®, 1966. Why do lyrics to bubble-gum songs adhere to my brain like bugs on flypaper?

252 This, you see, is one way Osama is thematically linked to our walker-about Steven. He's "having his way" with the ladies.

diet of villagers than whatever he's being fed now is difficult to parse. [We all know "everything wild tastes like chicken."] He's become the father of fine handbags, which brings us to the name question.

"Surely,"—oh, I can hear your mental gears grinding—"He *wasn't* named Osama in 1991!? Osama wasn't a suitably scary name until a decade later!"

That's what I love about my readers. Always thinking.

You're on the money. In 1991 the villagers called the croc "John Major," naming him for the then-Prime Minister of Great Britain, which suggests something intriguing about the views of the inhabitants of a remote Ugandan village concerning the Brits.

John Major [the croc] was re-christened Osama[253] for more obvious reasons after the calamitous events of 9/11. This certainly suggests that, remote or not, the denizens of Luganga follow world news. [They also presumably knew that Tony Blair had succeeded Major—but Tony is a tiger, not a crocodile.]

Here's the thing, this father of fine handbags is no longer a terrorist so what I'm suggesting here is that he should be renamed again. I vote for Hermes®. Hermes® crocodile-skin purses fetch about $65K apiece. (!) [You can look it up! I did.]

And here we find a second possible link between the wounded Mr. Goolsby—recovering nicely thanks to the more than tender and very enthusiastically energetic care of Janet Keith, MSN, and humming the pop song footnoted on the previous page —and the monster croc. From here on out, I'm going to call him Hermes® regardless of the sensibilities of Uganda Croc LTD®'s management, and get this! The song/album *98.6—if you missed footnote 248*—was a <u>Mercury</u> Records® release! And the singer of that bit of bubblegum used the stage name "Keith."

Furthermore, Donley-Don, the Blackfella, was regaling Steven with tales of the Lizard Ancestor as they trod and a large croc is certainly somewhere in the same ballpark as *Megalania.*

Spooky or what? It all fits.

But, be that as it may, here's the point—and following his mishap with the Phoenix palm Steven sees himself as much too well versed in the points of things to listen in just now—big creatures loom large in our imaginations. Particularly big

---

253 Similar in a way to my renaming of Tammy Faye as Pomonella mentioned on page 140, or the shifting identity of Oreo AKA Snowflake AKA Sparrow née Ryder, my one-eyed wonder-cat.

creatures with claws and sharp pointy teeth.[254]

Yet the likelihood of our consumption by such a beast is actually pretty low. Even in Luganga, during ~~Osama's~~ Hermes' former reign of terror before he turned entrepreneurial, you had a nine in ten chance of *not* becoming today's blue plate special. For most of us in the glee club optimistically referred to as *Homo sapiens sapiens,* ending up inside a monster is something we'd have to work at: surfing in shark-infested waters or backpacking in lion country or messing with a grizzly for example.

You who are reading this are far more likely to be bitten by a chihuahua than a croc.

Meanwhile, for the incautious, here's a word to the wise from Queensland.

"Don't eat geckos."

A fellow there swallowed one of those little lizards on a bet in 2019 and died ten days later from some horrible something in his gut. [I'll spare you the symptoms. You can look it up if you're a glutton for such.] It seems Asian house geckos (*Hemidactylus frenatus*) harbor an insidious tape worm *(Cestoda sp.)* that upsets a human tummy something awful.

[Sometimes it's the little things in life that get you down. *Hemidactylus frenatus* tops out at about 6 inches.]

This gets us closer to the goal line in this little expedition. "What," we now ask ourselves, "Is the goal?" ["There *is* a goal?"]

"What," we also ask ourselves, "Is the connection between the philandering Mr. Goolsby—for philandering he was, in light of his years itemized with Terry, informal though the relationship may have been—the *Megalania, Crocodylus niloticus* (to give Hermes® his rightful name), not eating geckos, 9/11, 98.6 and, to circle back to the very first sentence, the *Procoptodon?*"

The connection, dear reader, is obvious.

But for those who don't do well at "reading between the lines" [sigh] I guess I'll have to come up with something.

Steven Goolsby is only in this story as a *vehicle*. I used him as a foil for Donley-Don's tale-telling, and threw in sex with the nurse practitioner to spice things up. People like stories with steamy sex scenes, which I thoughtfully provided. [Both in this gripping tale and in footnote 226. It leaves me a little breathless.]

What the story is "about" is the fact that while large scary

254 Reminding us, as it must, of the *Carcharodontosaurus* featured so magnificently in the story of that name in *Self-Evident: We Hold These Tooths,* BUB, 2021.

things with big teeth often feature in our nightmares, the really dangerous animals in our midst are bipedal. ~~Osama~~ Hermes®, for example, was perfectly happy nabbing a villager now and again, until he was wrangled. Oh, we might imagine that "three hots and a cot" and a harem of slithering bedmates would be just fine, but I bet he's bored as hell.

Megalania was perfectly happy lurking around Down Under until our team showed up and either killed them directly or killed off the *Procoptodons* that were a favorite snack item.

The man in Queensland was probably perfectly happy up until a "friend" bet him he wouldn't eat a gecko.

Meanwhile we in the U.S. were perfectly happy enjoying what we used to call "civil liberties," and hundreds of thousands of Iraqis and Afghanis were perfectly happy being alive right up until the other Osama gave the U.S. a great excuse to start bombing the Middle East back to the stone age, to coin a phrase.

Perhaps we ought to start calling Osama, the erstwhile student of the U.S. military (and ally in the oppo to the Russian occupation of Afghanistan) cum terrorist plotter of winged assault —Hermes? The herald of the gods he was also the protector of human heralds, travelers, thieves, merchants and orators. It's hard to argue that bin Laden didn't deliver a message, and maybe it came from the gods. [Ares comes to mind. And Dolos, the mythological personification of trickery, cunning deception, craftiness, treachery and guile.]

It kind of beggars one's thinking to consider how much more damage we've done to ourselves and the globe than was inflicted on our country in September of 2001. We fought a "war on terror" and we lost, big time. Seems to me we'd be way ahead today if we had simply, from the get-go, kept our hands off.

Dolos dared us and we swallowed the gecko, to coin another phrase. [Minty fresh, my coinage. Eh what?]

Oh, and I almost forgot to tell you: the *Procoptodon goliah* was a giant kangaroo! Is that cool, or what? Much favored as a snack by *Megalania* and the first human settlers in Australia. While a nearly 9' tall jumper weighing 500 pounds might have done some serious damage if it landed *on you,* they were herbivores and so posed no particular threat to *Homo sapiens sapiens.*

Nothing like the threat we pose to our own. IMHO.

~~Letting g~~...—No, *Really Letting Go*

You're getting another bit of insight into the creative process at this point, and perhaps you're thinking, "About damn time!" Hey, I get that. I really do. Here we are at the three-quarter mark, and you deserve a look behind the curtain. It's OK. I'm dressed. This isn't a shower curtain you're peeking past, by the by, though I might reassure you that like my "good eggs" I do bathe regularly.

You see up top that I came *this* close to once again pasting the title "Letting *go*" onto whatever oozes out down below, but I was strong. I resisted. In the *nick of time!*

Now the question becomes "who?" How 'bout we do the eeney, meeney, miney, mo thing, starting from the very beginning. OK? But first we need some ground rules. Do we go with syllables or words? Big diff! Twenty-nine syllables as I count them scattered amidst 23 words. Like Robert Frost's two roads diverging in a yellow wood, that is likely to make all the difference.

Saving you the trouble, and counting only the actual characters in this admittedly brilliant collection—as versus those mentioned referentially [Charles Dickens, Charles Mann, Joseph Banks, Capt. James Cook, Bruce Chatwin, Kamala Harris, and so on and so forth—that is to say, the "real" people] nor counting myself or anyone mentioned on the dedication page or in the Foreword, assuming I compose one—the 23rd name to pop out at us is that of Jim Pernal, one of the detectives who investigated the *Noblet®* caper.

The 28th name is that of David Dwyer, the Slick Wiccan Chicken® King, or maybe he'd prefer "Warlock?"

Thinking it through, I see that Pernal resurfaced when his partner was showing off his oh-so-cool obsidian knife,[255] so he's had a second slot. But Dwyer, when last we heard of him, was on the lam. Much more likely to be an interesting story there, and it's wrong to leave either a character or a reader hanging like that.

So we're going with the syllables which come to think of it, is what I did as a kid. E knee me knee my knee mo, etc. I guess I

255 You see what I mean? These keep popping up.

didn't first settle on a "rule," this all being kind of seat-of-the-pants.

So, Dave fled Asheville after the actual ingredients in Slick Wiccan Chicken® were brought to light by that [unnamed] DNA researcher at Western Carolina U. He was fleeing from the long arm of the Health Department as well as the longer arms of the local coven. If the superintendent of public health didn't put the fear of gods[256] in him, the keepers of the supernatural scared the bejeezus out of him.

Where shall we have him land?

I've got it. Canada! "O Canada!"[257]

O, this is going to be fun!

Dave, fortunately enough for our protagonist, held a valid Western Hemisphere travel initiative-compliant document. I don't know whether it was a U.S. passport, a U.S. passport card, an "enhanced" driver's license, or a Trusted Traveler® card. I do know it wasn't a military I.D. It's really kind of irrelevant, but look how much time I've saved you if you're thinking of escaping to the north! Lacking any of those you'll be turned away and your vacay will be spoiled. Rest assured, you will be grateful for this tip.

So Dave was holed up near a ski lodge in the Canadian Rockies at this point, and who should he bump into but Janet Keith? "It's a small world after all, it's a small world after all ... etc."

Well, well. We know how Dave ended up there, but Janet? Wasn't she in bed with Steven Goolsby in that hot and steamy scene on page 144? In Australia? How the heck did she get from a sheep station in the outback to the Canadian Rockies in five short pages?

I fear you're suffering under a misapprehension regarding timelines. These stories are not actually sequential, even if I drain them like cooked noodles from the ether in the order that they soften in my fevered brain. (About 8 minutes at a full boil.)

Let's think back. When was Janet all hot and bothered about Mr. Goolsby? It was, perhaps, two weeks after he went walkabout with Donley-Don, right? And ... come on now ... *think*.

That was a year and more *before* Terry returned stateside to assume management of the family farm, which was a year and a half before she quit working at Hickory Nut Gap Farm®, which was a good long while *before* my dental appointment that caused

256 As a reminder, there are no gods.

257 You can practically hear Joni singing "I could drink a case of you."

my intersection with Terry's herd, her invitation to lunch, and our imaginary love affair, which probably would have gone on for some time before we cooled off ... oh, my, it would have been blissfully hot and heavy.Oh, how we would have gone at it![258]

Have I made my point? Five pages can cover a lot of ground. So even if Janet and Steven were "itemized" for a while Down Under, she's had plenty of time to wind up the affair and her stint in Australia's universal single-payer Medicare system and go home to Canada.

Down Under to up-over. This sort of adventure is not uncommon for citizens of the Commonwealth. "Have a bit of a go," as some say.

Colleen? If you're reading this, thank you. Thank you. It was, what, the early 70s? When you inserted that colloquialism into my worldview. Remember? You said your Mom was a "bit of a goer." I'd never heard the term, but I knew she did the hoochy-koochy for certain! Or the hanky-panky, as the case might be.

Colleen, by the by, is a real person, so we won't count her if we do the "E knee" thing again. She's an old friend who currently dwells somewhere in Calgary. [She's on Facebook and if you send her a friend request, go ahead and blame me.] A real live Canadian. Anyway, you just never know when something someone says to you will come in handy, do you?

It's like the word "antimacassar." This one I can't quite pinpoint. As to where I first heard it, I mean. Or from whom. But fortunately it was part of my lexicon before page 114, else I might have imagined that it involved Aboriginals who shunned trade, rather than a protective covering for the back of a chair. This stuff comes in handy! [As does an antimacassar if you've moved on from salamanders to some sort of clawed companion animal.]

Fortunately Dave was able to get a work permit after he got a job offer from a fried chicken restaurateur in Banff.[259] Janet, being a nurse practitioner, had no trouble finding work on her return home. "Ski resort" says it all. Lots of patching up to do.

But wait. How did they meet? With something like 10,000 residents and heaven knows how many tourists, Banff is not a village in the Outback by any stretch.

Ah. That's it!

I forgot. I let Dave read a draft of that story about Mel somewhere upslope. I figured Dave knew a thing or two about the

258 Note how I repeatedly insert these sex scenes to titillate my readers!
259 I chose Banff because it's fun to say.

fried chicken biz and that he'd be able to help me lend a bit of verisimilitude to my patter. Which he did. Originally I didn't have Mel peering out through the slot in the wall, rather it was around a corner in the walk-thru from sales area to kitchen. The slot thing was Dave's idea. [If your protagonists aren't able to helpout once in a while ... why bother with them? That's my rule.]

So Dave read about Mel's show offy trick with the wet arm reaching into the vat of boiling oil to grab a leg or a wing. [Which, I'll remind you, I recommended you *not* try at home.][260]

But Dave didn't pay attention to the part about using a f*rozen* piece of chicken. Tut. Tut. He reached in to grab a thigh[261] that not only had been in the fryer for a considerable time, but had been *thawed* before immersion.

Burned? You better believe it!

The boss insisted he head down to the Alpine Medical Clinic®.[262] Canadians are very keen on health care, eh what?

Well, let's just say it was love at first sight.

For Dave.

Janet? Not so much. I mean, Dave *seemed* OK. It was more than obvious that he bathes regularly, for instance. He speaks in whole sentences. He's got dimples. A lot of the right stuff, if you see what I'm saying. Then again, she could tell his metaphorical tongue was hanging out when she walked into the examining room, which may or may not have been a good sign.

She was relieved that he didn't grope her, something that happens way too often to female medical personnel alone in a small room with a man. Just sayin'. [Hey, guys. Come on! Shape up or ship out!]

But, really? He reached into a fryer full of hot grease? Was he nuts? ["Jesus Murphy! Is this bloke a few clicks short of a round trip, or what?"]

She spread some ointment, wrapped Dave's hand and gave him a scrip for a non-narcotic analgesic. After his exit she shook her head. ["These Yanks. Next around he'll be riding a moose."[263]] To be clear, no encouragement had been given.

But Dave was smit and persisted. He sent her flowers via the clinic address. He sent her a Heritage Day[264] card in the first

260 The legal team here is very keen on avoiding this kind of exposure.

261 Another sex reference? Could be. Certainly hot!

262 A real place. I like for my fictional characters to have real jobs.

263 Trying to make Janet sound Canadian. How'm I doin'?

264 A real holiday in Alberta. See how I roll?

week of August. He invited her to dinner at the Eden®.[265]

He seemed serious! C$110 for a three-course? C$192 paired with wines? C$384 plus tip for a couple? Why not?

The meal was delicious, Dave proved to be great good fun, and the evening ended all too soon. When Janet dropped him off [he doesn't have a car yet] she told him, "Thanks ever so. I was wrong about you."

That left him thinking.

That's when he really let go![266]

O Canada!

265 A real restaurant in Banff. Accuracy is essential!

266 Leading to the night a month or so later, *sans* gotch!. … *Embuée! Embuée! Embuée!*

Sans Gotch

I imagine that last footnote left some of you mystified. The French “without” coupled with an unfamiliar term. At least unfamiliar to non-Canucks.

Up north they call a pair of men's underwear a gotch. And e*mbuée* is the feminine form of “steamy” *en langue française.*

You see what you missed? I put these explicit and lurid sex scenes in here to keep readers on the edges of their seats. Panting. Hearts racing. People who sit around all day reading don't get enough exercise as a general rule and bumping up your pulse rate every so often is my way of tending to your cardiac fitness. Can I get a thank you?

As I write *these very words*[267] ancient mummies of Egypt's royal pharaohs are preparing to emerge from their century-long resting places and parade through the streets of Cairo in search of a new home.

If that doesn't fire up your imagination I don't know what will! And every last one of them is pretty certainly *sans* gotch, insofar as gotches hadn't been invented in the high and far off time when this crowd was shrink-wrapped.

The mummies of Ramses the Great and 21 of his fellow rulers are taking part in what is being billed as "The Pharaoh's Golden Parade," a highly anticipated event organized by the Egyptian Ministry of Tourism and Antiquities®—appropriately on Easter weekend, since the dead are being raised.

Eighteen kings and four queens of Egypt, along with their coffins and whatnots and so-forths are being moved from their old home at The Egyptian Museum® to their new high-tech resting place at the vaunted National Museum of Egyptian Civilization®.[268]

At first Alice[269] had wanted to attend the hoedown, despite the difficulties and threat posed by the pandemic. For one thing

267 Exactly 8:40 a.m. EDT, April 3, 2021

268 This is a very real thing happening today, as we speak. Think of this as short story *vérité.*

269 Remember Alice? We talked about her fascination with all things Egypt on page 133.

she's not gotten the vaccine yet and the possible exposure seemed daunting. But when she saw pics of the vehicles the pharaoh's had lined up for the 5-mile ride, she realized that spectators wouldn't actually be seeing "them:" They would basically be looking at floats [think Rose Bowl®]. So she's decided to hold off until the star performers are settled in their new glass cases with temperature-controlled nitrogen atmosphere and bordered with blow-up X-rays of the shrink-wrapped mummies—some future time when, hopefully, the current fever dream (i.e. this time of cholera) has subsided.

In the event, she was proved right. Even locals had trouble seeing the pageant. It was a made-for-TV affair with large shielding screens erected all along the route so the cameras wouldn't show pictures of the surrounding slums. Those who tried to peer around the barricades were shooed away by security guards who told them to watch it on their phones.

'Nuff said. We've already done a deep dive into Alice's life, so we'll set her aside.

I've heard from several of you that you think I've given Greta short shrift, and looking back, I've got to agree. It does seem kind of rude to have had her arrested, booked, convicted, jailed for, what? Four whole hours? Then ... nothing?

Oh, right. We had her acquitted and later that nice juror, Ellen Fulton, sent her a card by way of apology on page 38.

Of course we insinuated that she was involved in a 4-way between Egyptian cotton sheets [she was] and spun off with Geoff. However, we've skated right past her "inner life."

It seems kind of a shame. I mean, to have invented a person and then overlooked the richness of that individual's core. For "core" there surely must be, whether that "being" is a good apple or a bad one. [Notice I've switched metaphors here. Talking about the "core" of a good or bad egg would be a bad yolk.] [Oh, I crack me up sometimes!]

So, what is it that so intrigues us about Greta Strenberg?

Who is it that looks back at her from the morning mirror?

That's the kind of question I expect from a reader of your caliber. It's the kind of thing that makes my life worthwhile.

[Thank you very much.]

"Strenberg," (as she calls herself) "is all about nuts."

Damn, we didn't see this one coming, did we?

"Strenberg," she says to her mirror each morning, "Nuts!"

[Nor is she referring to nuts in gotches. FYI.]

"T-nuts, lug nuts, lock nuts, hex nuts, cup nuts, cap nuts, square nuts, ring nuts, capstan nuts, wing nuts, Grape-nuts® ... the works." Oh boy, can she rattle that off. She's got a diverse collection on a bookshelf in her bedroom! [Like Egyptian cotton we note, these involve threads.] [Except the latter.[270]]

Nor does she limit herself to the heavy metal world! "Cashew, peanut, macadamia, walnut, chestnut, hazelnut, pecan, pistachio, almond, Brazil, kola, cacao and pine! Whooee!" These she doesn't collect, but rather consumes. She'll buy a bag of cashews at the co-op and gobble them over ensuing days or weeks, then peanuts, then macadamias, etc. and so forth, running through the list and then starting at the top again. [Unlike Egyptian cotton, these are not threaded.]

Oh, geez. *Macadamias?* (Italics mine.) When was the last time? My heart cries out, "Perfidia."

You see what I mean? We make all kinds of assumptions about the people we meet but there are depths we don't often plumb. There are elements much too easily overlooked.

Just imagine it. Combing her hair in the morning, in front of the mirror. "T-nuts, lug nuts, lock nuts, hex nuts ..." You see what I mean? Brushing her teeth, "Cashew, peanut, macadamia, walnut ..." etc. The woman is very, very deep. Into nuts.

But this story isn't about that. No, not at all, though I think it does afford us a peek under the hood. There's a lot going on in her squirrel cage of a brain.

This little "Iditarod" two-step, to cast it in an icy heroic Arctic expanse, is about "what Greta did" when she was shopping for shoes. Is there any effort more fraught?

"No" is the correct answer.

She started out in her retail endeavor "early," meaning at 10 a.m. when stores open. She visited all the "usual suspects" in the city. From the family-owned local vendor downtown to the chain shops in and around the mall to two discount outlets out on the fringes. At first blush her footware framework did not appear all that complicated. Comfort. (Obviously.) Durability. (Ditto.)

Color.

Oh dear. There's the rub. She had in mind a certain shade of blue. A very particularly specific shade of blue.

[I kind of wish my protagonists were less picky.]

---

270 Did you know there's been a nationwide shortage of Grape-nuts® during the time of cholera? Really. And people were paying up to $120 per box! Is that nuts, or what?

So, here's the thing. Greta is expecting to find a pair of comfortable shoes that appear to be solidly made that match! ... that match! That match! Her vest!

What? What vest?

The *stylish* vest she sewed up for herself out of synthetic chamois cloth[271] (with a satin lining) is Cadet Blue 2 on a color chart. This is slightly darker than Celeste or Paled Turquoise, perhaps the same intensity as Light Turquoise only a hair bluer and not with the slight tinge of gray you see in Cadet Blue 3. If you want to get a good mental picture, um, think of Light Sky Blue 2 only with a few drops of aqua thrown in.

All of us who've shopped for Cadet Blue 2 shoes are quite familiar with her dilemma. They are *very hard to find* and when your local retailer, say Shoe Show® or Sole Survivors® or Tar Heels® receives a shipping container load of the things they fly out the door as if they were winged like Hermes' *ταλαριά*.[272]

Like worms gobbled up by early bird shoppers.

Like ants slurped up by hungry pangolins.[273]

In any event, here we've arrived at the nubbin.

Why is Greta so attached to Cadet Blue 2? We know she is because, hey, that's what she purchased at JoAnn Fabrics® to use for her stitchery, and there were many, many options. We see her in shoe shop after shoe shop carrying likely pairs to the front of the store to compare tints–shoe:vest– in natural light, then shaking her head in disappointment.

For that matter why do you prefer red tomato juice?[274] Which, if you are a tomato juice drinker, I would bet dollars to donuts you prefer to, say, *brown* tomato juice. Right? Yet, if you'd never *seen* red tomato juice the brown "natural" juice would seem completely normal. It's not like we don't drink brown cola or cocoa. And that clear Coke® they're peddling in Japan? I don't think so. Who are they trying to fool, anyway?

Or why do some people absolutely refuse to purchase a green car? This had serious repercussions for Saab®, all of whose cars were bottle green until sometime in the 1950s (WWII military surplus plasticized green paint was cheap). Though one

271 Have you noticed that this is the second reference to "synthetic" chamois cloth—see page 64—indicating that no animals were skinned in preparing these stories. I find that enormously admirable.

272 Yes, Greek. You know, his sandals?

273 "Pangolin" is almost as much fun to say as "niblick," COVID or no.

274 Red tomato juice is artificially colored.

would imagine that Swedes would rather have a green car they can locate after a snowstorm than, say, a white one.

There's been quite a bit of research conducted concerning why we have favorite colors, particularly trying to tease out whether a preference is innate or learned. There is an argument to be made that evolutionary success might have played a role. Fruits generally deepen in color when they are ripe, for example. Green apples might give one a tummy ache, and rotten apples are brown. Green berries are often unpalatable, while red or blue ones are just right. Except for the red ones that are toxic.

Others have argued that blue skies mean good weather, so sky blue might be associated with pleasant memories, though not so much if you are trying to grow edibles during a drought. Meanwhile, researchers have managed to put together a kind of color wheel of cultural favorites and then discovered that faves differ from country to country, fueling the idea that it is nurture, not nature.

Still, what ist it about this “Cadet Blue 2” thing that has our protagonist so fixated? We might note here that she has no idea that it is called “Cadet Blue 2,” only that she likes the color. When you stop and think about it, which I urge you to do right now, what can it be?

Those of you who think it had something to do with a love interest can move to the head of the class, and the thing is, Greta doesn't even understand that because it goes back such a long way. You see, she had a crush (aw!) on Brent Croman in high school, her first real “fell for” heartthrob of a crush, and she hasn't thought about him in years. It never amounted to much.

Oh, they went out a few times but the truth of the matter is that he was considerably more interested in himself than in pairing off. When she was in the first blush of infatuation, though, she was greatly taken by his performance on the basketball court! The school team color was ... yep. Cadet Blue 2. So Greta, without remembering much about either Brent or the school colors, has a strong attraction to a color associated with good feelings from the past. Back before life got so damn complicated.

I suggested that she find a pair of shoes that were in the Blue Cadet 2 range but a more commonly available color. Say Kentucky Sky® or Sapphire Blue® from Rit®, and simply dye the vest to match the shoes.

Greta burst into tears. "You don't understand," she sobbed. When the immediate emotion faded she became quite peeved with me. "I've about had it with you, Bothwell. Telling tales about me, my love life, my *Noblet*®, my squirrel cage."

"OK, OK. Don't get your gotches in a twist!"

"Crumbling" — continued from page 142

[Note: I didn't have room on the above-mentioned page to indicate that this story was continued here, so if you've found this exciting conclusion, congratulations! You did it on your own!]

"Surely," I hear you thinking, "Surely dealing with a few tough math questions on a standardized test doesn't qualify as a "life-changing" incident."

Maybe not for you. But End of Grade or End of Class tests have done immeasurable damage to the psyches of a generation that has labored under the iron fist of No Child Left Behind. Fact.

On the other hand, as noted, memory is uncertain. As noted elsewhere, everybody lies. So let's peel this Larry "onion" just a bit.

Aha! I dug around in his desk while he was walking his basset and I found the test results! He may have been kind of "stumped," but he still got enough answers right to end up in the high 90s. So, you're right.

What then? What soul-searing event in Larry's life made him what he is?

You are not going to believe this. I mean, you obviously need to take everything you've read here with a grain of salt, but this is the sorry truth, and I'm afraid it is my duty to report it.

We're right back to Franklin Franklin. Didn't see this coming. Didn't plan on it. Wouldn't hope for it. Almost can't imagine it. Hate to believe it. Thought it wouldn't come to this. Sort of thought we'd not hear anything about him again, being a bad egg and all. Presumed he was out of the "big picture" at this point, and would no longer intrude.

How I could have been so wrong is a puzzlement. But, in fact, and you've seen how important facts are to me, the big event in Larry's life, the thing that knocked his socks off, left him gasping for air, bewitched, bothered, bewildered ... was reading "Sew True Cedes." [Page 13.]

Really. Absolutely.

He'd bought "organic" chestnuts from Franklin as well.

He is devastated. His faith in humanity? Crumbling.

Cashing In

Mixed meaning there, eh? [I find myself using the Canadian "eh" quite frequently since our little *affaire du cœur* in Banff. O Canada! O Canada! "I could drink a case of you," etc.]

Cashing in can go one of two ways. In the first instance it can be synonymous with "cashing out." Selling something that has gained in value or popularity is to "cash in" on an opportunity that has reared its attractive little noggin.

But it can also suggest giving up, as in "I can't keep my eyes open another minute. Time to cash in."

Another song just floated through my multitasking brain, so, this:

> "Sunset is an angel weeping, holding out a bloody sword,
> No matter how I squint I cannot, make out what it's
> pointing toward ..."[275]

You can see right off how that would distract.

[What *is* it pointing toward, anyway?]

Say, f'rinstance, you've won a pile of chips at Monte Carlo —not that I'm in any way endorsing gambling (the house always wins in the end). You take the chips to the cashier's cage and you cash out, which is, obviously, also "cashing in."

Yet, here's the thing—or, more likely, "a" thing—when you can't keep your eyes open you are very likely to say, "Time to cash in" when, actually, it would be more apropos to say, "Time to cash out."

See what I mean?

> "Sometimes you feel like you've lived too long
> Days drip slowly down the page ..."[276]

Where was I? Oh, right. Brent Croman. There was a casher in if ever I've known one. If ever.

---

275 "Pacing the Cage," Bruce Cockburn, from the album *The Charity of Night,* Golden Mountain Music, 1997

276 Ibid.

He was pretty insufferable back in high school, and Greta is lucky that he was "one that got away." But hard knocks do sometimes knock some sense into a person and Brent "grew up."

They say, "Winning isn't everything but losing isn't anything." However, losing is actually "something" so "they" are wrong. You can quote me on that.

Think about it. Losing weight for example. A lot of people want to do that and some succeed. Losing your shirt. A lot of people don't want to do that and some manage not to. Others want someone else to do that—usually men, in my experience, regarding women. And here we have another steamy sex scene.

Do I hear a thankyou?

If you're reading a used copy of the current collection I'd bet dollars to donuts[277] that the upper left corner of this page is dog-eared like in those James Bond novels we passed around in junior high, back in the day—marking "those" pages.

Just imagine someone "losing her shirt?" OMG!

Or if you're a woman, "losing his shirt," if he's pretty fit.

Or, one or the other if you're that way.

Brent experienced the right amount of loss along the way and now, in his 40s, is much less insufferable. He's come to realize that he isn't the center of the universe.

Thought you'd want to know.

This story, however, is headed elsewhere. A number of you have indicated interest in the "unnamed" biologist mentioned on pages 55 and 149. "What drew him to do a DNA test on Slick Wiccan Chicken®?"[278]

Reading the preceding footnote I see that his name is Grover Hanson. So, what's the deal with Grover?

Gro has a Ph.D. in genetics! Wowza!

He's been doing research regarding salamanders!

Leading us to wonder if he's acquainted with Larry Morris, and darned if he isn't. Remember, Larry has a biology degree, although some *contretemps* with Deb shifted him to bike repair and, connecting the dots, we now learn that he studied with

---

277 I realize it's pretty lame to use the same tired expression twice in just four pages, but that just seems to be how I roll. And this is the third time I've leaned on it in this collection. I'll try to do better.

278 Full disclosure: While it's true that any number of readers have asked about Grover Hanson, to give him a name at this point, the principal reason I'm returning to him is in order to repeat "Slick Wiccan Chicken®" which amuses me no end. Colonel Sanders move over!

Gro at Western. [By now, perhaps, you are beginning to realize that when I concoct a scenario I try to make it "whole."]

Deborah, by the way, had a brief fling with Gro after she and Larry parted, which was one of the things that stung: Why she'd prefer another salamander commander [couldn't pass up the alliteration, sorry] who seemed blander, not grander, [OK, enough already] quite confused Larry, who confronted Deb once, a few months later. "Why him?"

"Who?" was a logical response, since Larry hadn't attached a name to the query.

"Grover."

"Oh, him. Yeah, you're right." [They'd already broken up.]

So, anyway, while Gro's serious research has involved salamanders in recent years, his hobby involves DNA sequencing of this and that. He's tested all sorts of things: pastrami, celery, freshwater mussels, cats, olive oil, the office aspidistra ... you name it. When he saw an ad for Slick Wiccan Chicken® with its odd assortment of ingredients, he recognized a serious challenge.

What I wanted to tell you, though, is ...

> "I've proven who I am so many times, the magnetic strip's worn thin ..."

Sorry, that earworm keeps popping up.

But I wanted to tell you what happened to Gro just yesterday.[279] He was cycling home from the lab and he saw an *amazing* event. It really blew him away! It was the kind of thing that leaves one just shaking one's head in near disbelief.

I can only think that you'd have reacted the same way if you'd been on his pedals—to coin a phrase. Or on his saddle, to use the proper term for "bike seat."

In the same way one might react to, oh, I don't know, a David Copperfield® trick where a tiger disappears—I mean in person, not in a video which is so very easy to "fake"—or, perhaps, let me think ... oh, I know, perhaps seeing little green men fixing a flat on a flying saucer. You know?

That would be a real surprise, wouldn't it now? Did you even *know* that those things had wheels? It suggests that they have to taxi or something, when I'm pretty sure we all imagine that they operate with some sort of antigravity thing where they just go up and down. Right?

---

279 April 9, 2021

Well, anyway, Grover Hanson was really, really stunned. When he got home he had to tell Snook [*la gata*] about it. Twice.

Ariel and Snook many and many a year ago.
[All of the cats in my stories are real former companions of mine]

Cashing in again

Heh heh. Fooled you on that last one didn't I? Kind of left you hanging.

That was intentional. The idea was to get you to continue to this page, which you have just done, thinking that you'd learn what Gro saw that so astonished him.

Maybe you will and maybe you won't. But the thing is, you're now deeply engrossed in another story and don't really have an easy out. So we'll get back to our DNA researcher in a few, but for the nonce we're going to check in with Deb.

She's one of the more significant characters in this book, given that she's had romantic flings with two of our protagonists. So far I'm pretty sure there have only been six such, not counting Terry with whom my *romance torride*[280] was admittedly fictive. Of course it's probable that others have had more than one "significant other" over time, but if so, we've not yet heard.

Oh, and by the by, Deb is the person who showed Gro the ad for Slick Wiccan Chicken®, so you see?

Deb is from Kansas, which I think explains a lot.

I realize this raises all sorts of questions, so right off the bat[281] we should learn what she "does."

She whistles.

Deb found a job commensurate with her biology degree after graduation, working for Animal Control in Cullowhee, which principally involves dog-catching. [And here you thought "whistling" was some kind of hobby? Dog whistle. Dog whistle.]

However the more interesting elements in her line of work involve species other than *Canis lupus familiaris*. She's had to collect snakes, bats, possums, raccoons, ferrets, rabbits, lizards, a monkey ... a monkey! Oh, and wolf spiders.

You'd be surprised how often people are so petrified of a large spider that they call animal control. I mean, really? I can kind of see where one of those giant bird-eating tarantulas would freak someone out, being a foot long and weighing as much as a

280 I realize we haven't used *la langue française* for a bit. Didn't want you to get rusty.

281 Whence "wool of bat" derives.

small puppy, but wolf spiders? Nah. "Wolf spiders are members of the family *Lycosidae*, from the Ancient Greek word "λύκος" meaning "wolf". They are robust and agile hunters with excellent eyesight. They live mostly in solitude and hunt alone, and do not spin webs. Some are opportunistic hunters pouncing upon prey as they find it or even chasing it over short distances. Some wait for passing prey in or near the mouth of a burrow."[282]

Deb, by the way, enjoys saying a Greek word as much as we do. "λύκος," she'll intone as she plucks the little *Lycosidae* from the wall and drops it into a pint jar, impressing the frightened homeowner with her derring do as well as her language skills. *"Araignée,"*[283] she sometimes adds, kind of showing off. *"Spinne,"*[284] she'll say with a casual laugh.

[Sometimes I think it would be wonderful to be referred to as "robust and agile." That is so "me."]

So here's what I wanted to tell you about Deb.

She's 5'6".

Most likely, though, you want to know about the monkey. Am I right? If you're like me that probably brings to mind either John Lennon® or Barenaked Ladies®, the latter suggesting removal of shirts, of course.

Your assignment is to compare and contrast.

"Everybody's got something to hide except for me and my monkey," VS. "If I had a million dollars I'd buy you a monkey."

See?

Brenda Ellington thought owning a squirrel monkey was a good thing. Some people are *that way*. What she didn't really appreciate was how darned clever those elfin critters are or how hard they can bite when angered. Word to the wise: if you insist on owning a squirrel monkey, *don't make the little guy mad*. OK?

So, Brenda's monkey, named Alphonse by the way, got out of the house one day when she was at work, and traipsed over to the neighbor's place. Jan Bender went into her kitchen and there was Alphonse eating handfuls of the pumpkin pie she'd left on the counter to cool.

"Shoo!" she said. Etc. Alphonse looked at her and shrugged, then continued enjoying dessert.

282 This from our friends at Wikipedia®.

283 *Française*

284 *Deutsche,* oh, we could go on and on.

Deb, who is very patient and kind, was able to collect the critter without much fuss. Alphonse had eaten his fill by the time she arrived and hopped up on her shoulder.

What Gro saw, to get back to the previous *contretemps,* was considerably more surprising than finding a squirrel monkey in your kitchen, though there are probably very few things more "out of the ordinary" than that. The next level might be finding a 14-foot-long anaconda in your bathtub, or, I don't know, arriving home to find a bare naked lady on your back deck, like Chester?

Remember Chester? From "Tummy Tuck," the back story regarding Lurlene the nudist? Oh, come on. You know. In *Waist Not, Want Knot?* Right? Chester hasn't forgotten, that's for sure.

You people.

So, when we last checked in with Gro he was cycling home from the lab when what should he see? [This is going to blow your mind!]

Right there, at the corner of Central Dr. and Old Cullowhee Road, Gro saw a *very, very* elderly woman helping a Boy Scout® cross the street! Can you imagine?

Peel me from the pavement!

"Sometimes the best map will not guide you
You can't see what's round the bend
Sometimes the road leads through dark places
Sometimes the darkness is your friend"[285]

---

285 "Pacing the cage." Cockburn. Earworm. Speaking of which, have you ever called Animal Control concerning an earworm? Nor have I. But this time, maybe.

Throwing in the sponge

I was just now reading about tapeworms, because why not? *Tetragonoporus calyptocephalus.* That'll make you think. You read the prefix "tetra" and you probably picture those little colorful aquarium fish. I did. But no. Up to 100' long! Inside a whale! OMG!

What I'm hearing just now, from that fellow in the back of the class, is something to the effect that throwing in the sponge is the same as throwing in the towel, and who do I think I'm fooling. I believe we'll just have to agree to disagree on this one.

For one thing, every sponge [Genus *Porifera*[286]] *I've* ever thrown has bounced. That's not something a towel would do. Not on a bet.

They are worlds apart ... and yet ... and yet. I will concede that both phrases came from the world of boxing and they both are used in the sense of giving up when one knows winning isn't possible. Both eyes blackened, some blood running down from one ear, chin having been taken on. But I will only concede *that* if you in the back will agree that boxing, like golf, is not a sport.

Do I hear a yes?

And that Dylan's song about Hurricane Carter is a no-go?

Yes again? Good.

I think we're going to get along just fine here.

Grover, in my view, has been a very important figure in this, what shall we call it? This steaming heap? If we look back we see that his "hobby" upended a chicken pot pie entrepreneur, he was a teacher to Larry of salamander husbandry fame, he had a brief hot and heavy with Deb ... and he watched in utter amazement as an old, old woman helped a Boy Scout® from curb to shining curb. Gosh, I'm tempted to go back and put him on the *Noblet®* jury. That would be *so* fitting!

---

286 These living fossils are ideal for studying the principal features of metazoans, such as extracellular matrix interactions, signal-receptor systems, nervous or sensory systems, and primitive immune systems. Thus, sponges are useful tools with which to study early animal evolution. They appeared approximately 580 million years ago. [Per our friends at Wikipedia®.] A very long way from "towels."

But no. He lives two counties over. There are enough attemps to rewrite history by those with questionable agendas and my aim is true. [Like, I'd note, Elvis Costello's.]

Here's one thing about Gro that you don't know.

He's never gotten over *Gravity's Rainbow*. Have you?

Didn't think so. That one went to the mat with me. And won. Honestly, it was kind of like David Foster Wallace's *Infinite Jest,*[287] you know? A little "too-too?" A little *inconfortable?*

So between DNA samples Gro worries about V-2's.

When students figure this out—oh, they do, they do—and begin to shout "Incoming!" at odd moments during the day, with a downward arcing whistle, Gro experiences a profound "fight or flight" response, with "flight" being the predominant reaction. "Fighting" an incoming rocket is not really a "thing."

If it were, for instance, a thrown obsidian knife,[288] well then, sure. Dodging is a thing and a knife can be thrown back. But no one dodges a V-2. Oh, I've known those who dodge a V8®—particularly when they discover it's artificially colored—or even a V8 Dodge®, every bit as repellent to some as the veggie juice.

My Dodge was a flathead six, FYI.

Hell of a good truck, now that the old memory track has been triggered. Don't recall where that beast landed. As was my previous ride, a Plymouth Special Deluxe®. Well, no, my previous previous. And what a loss! I never should have loaned my 1948 Plymouth Special Deluxe® to my brother, RIP.[289]

He didn't know a dipstick from a wiper blade.

Really, think what that one would be worth now?

Oh, dude! A lot!

I really can't decide whether Pynchon was deep or deceptive. A *poseur?* And who is he hiding from, anyway?

When you write things like, "There is nothing so loathsome as a sentimental surrealist," you beg a very long list of questions and owe us some answers.

For example the question posed by Wernher Von Braun in Tom Lehrer's memorable ditty "Wernher von braun."

"Vonce zey go up who kerss vere zey come down?"

When I stumbled on Pynchon's ascerbic comment regarding surrealists I have to admit I was puzzled. The sentimental among them may *in fact* be loathsome, but I have

287 See page 101.

288 See what I mean?

289 Yeah. Right. Irony upon irony. Both brother and Plymouth.

never personally run into one who exhibited much of any sentiment at all. Have you? You see?

Dali, for example, with his recommended diet of sea urchins: Or his admonition that one must hold the clear little marble from the eye of a fish under one's tongue as one begins to paint? This is about as "matter of fact" as one can swing.

Anyway, Gro is a bundle of nerves. That was a principal factor in Deb's need to get away: He's jumpy as hell. Spiders drive him wild, which seems kind of strange in a biologist if you ask me. And ticks?

One night, just as the pair were falling asleep post-diddle,[290] Gro bolted upright. "A tick! A tick!" He insisted she do a full body search and, of course, there was no tick. He had experienced a hypnagogic jerk. As a one-off that wouldn't have mattered much, but night after night?

I don't think so. Not that it was always a "tick."

"A spider! A spider!"

"A centipede! A centipede!"

"A wombat! A wombat!"

"A cane toad! A cane toad!"

"A V-2! A V-2!"

"A *Tetragonoporus calyptocephalus!*"

That was the worm that broke the camel's back, to coin a phrase. As a biology major herself, Deb knew *exactly* what that was, and afterward she couldn't sleep. While she's cool as a cucumber regarding most of the animal kingdom, tapeworms unsettle her. The idea of an invader living in one's gut makes her feel deeply queasy, and she tossed and turned the rest of the night. Two days later she threw in the sponge.[291]

[Oh, and to clear things up further, Deb talked a lot about tapeworms when she was itemized with Larry, which made him feel even more queasy than she and turned him from a career in biologic science to a career in bicycle engineering, though he later took up breeding salamanders. Tapeworms in amphibians pass through an intermediate crustacean host[292] so, to be on the safe side, Larry doesn't feed his crowd the latter.]

---

290 Chalk up another one. Whooey!

291 Here I think the difference between throwing in a towel and a sponge is clear. No biology graduate would ever consider the former.

292 The type of "inside scoop" you've come to expect from me. There are few "scoops" more consistently "inside" than tapeworms, IMHO.

~~Erased~~ Toad Away

First off, I didn't have room on the previous page to mention this and I didn't want to run over and end up with a mostly blank page 169.[293] But a word of advice: *Don't* call animal control if you have a tapeworm. OK?

So no tapeworms, pretty clearly a no-go with earworms, and you surely don't want your earthworms removed. Got it?

Also, as you'll note above, this story was almost going to called "Erased," which we can easily understand fits within our "cede" rubric. But Gro's shouting "cane toad!" just as Deb was drifting off one night led me to consider that you may not know why they can be so damn frightening.

While you're not eating geckos[294] it would also be a good idea to steer clear of eating cane toads *(Rhinella marina).* Better yet, don't even play with them. Think about Northern quolls.[295]

See?

I mean, even if they look *really tasty?* Even if you have, like, a whole knot? Don't. [Someday you'll thank me for this.]

There you go. However we were getting back to Jan Bender, weren't we? The pie chef whose recent pumpkin production was substantially consumed by a squirrel monkey? That's the kind of thing that can really unmake your day. Not to the same degree as, say, consumption of a cane toad, but still. You put considerable time and effort and energy into baking a nice pumpkin custard pie and then some sneaky little monkey slips in and gets all handsy with it? No wonder Jan was dejected.

This goes considerably beyond where it would land if she'd simply, say, used canned pumpkin and a frozen pie shell, you see? She *grew* the pumpkin, all right? And it was one of only two, the other having been converted to jack-o'-lantern and subsequently composted, meaning that this one was singular. Not to mention—but here I mention it anyway—that *that* pie crust was also home-.

[How often can one get away with "that *that*" BTW?]

---

293 The last time I left most of a page 169 blank I suffered. Oh, I suffered.

294 See page 147.

295 *Dasyurus hallucatus.*

[Should the previous interjection have more properly been a footnote? The last time we used that *that*—on page 128—we paused for breath in between. This is the kind of thing that keeps *me* up at night. Tapeworms? Not so much.]

So, post monkey-thing, Jan was in the doldrums.

As so many do—and don't think we don't know who you are—Jan, despite her "diet," consoled herself by eating an entire pint of Ben & Jerry's®. Or maybe Edy's®.[296] Following which she kind of kicked herself for so-doing, a phrase which often makes us wonder.

Really? Kick yourself? Where exactly? "Kick myself in the butt?" Have you tried that? Was it effectively motivational? "No" is the correct answer, thank you very much.

The other thing, aside from "last pumpkin standing," is for whom the pie was baked. Right? So we ask, "For whom did Jan bake the pie?" After all, we learned just moments ago that she was on a "diet." A person on a "diet" is unlikely to bake a whole pie for her own self, right? Maybe a tart(but not the French kind) – not a whole pie. [Though we note that she *did* have a pint of whichever in the freezer, making her "diet" perhaps more of a good intention than a "thing."]

But, and here's an actual "thing," having a pint tucked away behind the frozen vegetables is kind of a *Secret Storm,* you know? Like that soap opera? A hidden habit. Maybe almost a self-dare. "I know it's there, but I am strong ..." until I'm not.

Whereas cooking a pumpkin and blenderizing it and adding milk and eggs and sugar and spices, and mixing up some flour and shortening and salt and boiling water (for which I have a wonderful recipe by the way, ask me after class) and rolling it out into a pie shell, adding the above-mentioned pumpkin melange and then baking it? Well, well. I think we can agree that this is more intentional than impulsive. Can we not?

Ending a second paragraph in a row with "not."

And now, a third.

But I see a hand up. "Quolls?"

Good to see that someone in the room is thinking. I mean, I kind of hoped you'd get there on your own, but asking is next best. It tells me that you're interested in learning.

Quolls are marsupials.

---

296 I don't think we need to know the brand. Ice cream. OK? And by the by, we are getting very close to the goal post at this point.

Where was I? Oh, for whom the pie bakes? It bakes for thee. It bakes for thee! [Sorry, that just came naturally.]

Actually, Jan had baked the pie for ...

Another hand up? "Marsupial?"

Yes, like a kangaroo or a Tasmanian tiger.[297]

Larry.[298]

"What the hell does that have to do with cane toads?"

"Larry? I thought he was hooked up with Alice."

I can see you people aren't really interested in the parable of the pumpkin pie. So be it.

As for the second question: Read the damn footnote!

Regarding quolls and cane toads: As the BeeGees®, also sort of from Australia by the way, might have framed it, "It's a tragedy."[299]

To set the "record," so to speak, straight, the BeeGees® were only nominally "from" Australia—like cane toads—their family having moved there subsequent to their initial recording effort on their home turf, the Isle of Man (unlike cane toads).

When we turn that over in our musty minds—viz: Isle of Man—we must needs consider Manx cats, mustn't we? Of course we must.

As we've read in one of our previous collections[300] Manx cats inspired Pilates yoga, which isn't exactly yoga, but it's kind of similar. Actually, I mean, it inspired Pilates to invent Pilates. See?

So, like the BeeGees®, cane toads were "introduced" to Australia. Fortunately for Barry, Robin and Maurice, they weren't eaten by quolls. Unfortunately for the quolls they didn't read my warning on page 169.

Northern quolls are also known as the northern native cat, the north Australian native cat, the *satanellus* or *njanmak* in the

---

297 Page 118 and so forth. We are getting so close now!

298 Not the same Larry. FYI.

299 From "Tragedy," on the album *Spirits Having Flown,* RSO, 1979. Just one more now. Feeling all tingly.

300 Bingo! We've hit the long-sought golden ratio! (That ratio being the same as the ratio of the sum to the larger of the two quantities.) Oh, and where we read this before? I think it was in *Waist Not, Want Knot,* but it might have been in *Seize You on the Dark Side of the Moo.* I'm pretty sure it wasn't in either *Fifty Wheys to Love Your Liver* or *Self-Evident,* but things get kind of blurry at some point. Three fricking hundred footnotes! Is that amazing or what?

Indigenous Mayali language, *djabo* in Kunwinjke, and *wijingarri* in Wunambal, is a carnivorous marsupial native to Australia.[301]

See what happens after one hits the "magic number" of footnotes? Foreign languages begin to pop up like mushrooms after a rainstorm.

Sadly for the quolls, cane toads may take them the way of the thylacines.[302] CRISPR gene splicing could save them yet as I'm sure you know, but the outcome remains murky.

Anyway, Jan had baked the pie for Larry Monroe, her object of interest: "way to man's heart" and all that. Hence her saditude. Then, after eating the pint, sad again because the ice cream would have been a decent substitute for dessert, the pie being spoiled.

Why hadn't she thought of *that* before she picked up the fatal spoon? For fatal it proved. Though, obviously, we can't blame the ice cream: Eating it was her idea. [Though, honestly, I'm not clear that ice cream exactly caused her heart attack.]

To say that her expiry "wrecked the date" would be kind of an understatement.

When Larry arrived, bearing bouquet, Jan was way past giving a "cold shoulder." He found her there, on the kitchen floor, spoon in hand, carton nearby, stiffened like a post-cane toad quoll and clearly not the live-wire hookup of his dreams.

"Down I go
And I just can't take it all alone
I really should be holding you
Holding you
Loving you, loving you,
It's a tragedy."[303]

Poor guy.

---

301 This from Wikipedia. Sorry Klein. (See footnote 1.)

302 See page 118. And by the way, we are not going to rest on our footnote laurels. Onward and upward!

303 See footnote 299. The BeeGees®, by the by, wrote this just "goofing off" on the set while filming Sgt. Pepper's®. No.1 hit while "goofing off." Sigh. If only. I pine. I pine.

Erased

Looks like we're back on track now following our narrow escape from the cane toads. Close one.

"Let's hear it for the monkey!"[304]

I know this makes you think we're going to talk about Brenda Ellington now, being the squirrel monkey's ~~owner,~~ or rather, companion: She doesn't believe in "owning" an animal. Alphonse is more on the order of a close friend—such a dear when he isn't glad-handing a neighbor's pie or biting fingers.

But no. Brenda, sad to say, is an "extra" in this production and doesn't even have any speaking parts. As we well recall, she was at work when the whole monkey caper went down and obviously didn't know her merry monkey was missing until evening.

When she arrived home Jan's corpse was still on the kitchen floor [see page 195] and Brenda wouldn't know of her neighbor's demise for a few days. She did see the emergency vehicles arrive at one point, but she was too distraught to play the nosey neighbor card. For that matter, she didn't know about the pie until she read "Cashing in again."[305]

What we can surmise is that upon arriving home she grew frantic. She searched the house and found the open window. She called and called—which offers the possibility of, at least, a monologue. But no. We're learning of this in the aftermath.

The next morning, following a nearly sleepless night—and when she did sleep, a troubled sleep infested with anxiety dreams —she called Animal Control and was so relieved! She called in to

---

304 This is my favorite line from "Gitarzan" by Ray Stevens, and it seemed apropos given the scenes we just reviewed on pages 164 amd 169. No doubt you're scratching your head. "Why is our author inserting a reference to a Ray Stevens novelty number?" As I've been at pains to demonstrate, it all connects. Where was the last Tasmanian tiger seen? Tasmania, right? Okay. And Tasmania is the part of Australia closest to … come on … New Zealand, right? And where did "Gitarzan" do best? New Zealand! Where it reached #2 on the pop charts. See?

305 Page 163.

work to say she'd be late—another chance for some live chat? but no—and raced to the shelter to recover her naughty boy.

Anxiety dreams. This is where we were headed right up until the cane toads hopped into view.

Before we get into that, however, perhaps we should have a chat about toad-sucking. Toad-sucking is a "thing." You can look it up. And while the toad of choice among aficionados is *Bufo alvarius,* the Colorado river toad (sometimes also referred to as the Sonoran desert toad), those possessed of a bit more derring-do sometimes suck on cane toads. No, really.[306]

Secretions from the warty skin of these largish amphibians contain bufotenine AKA 5-MeO-DMT, a powerful hallucinogen.

The lesson here is "Suck?" Yes. "Consume?" No.

Mason Williams' performance of his clap-along poem, "Toad Suckers" appears on *The Listening Matter,* his 1964 album. Funny as the dickens. (You can look *that* up too.)

I think we might think of Grover's hypnagogic jerks[307] as a form of anxiety dream, but we would be wrong. They are more akin to hallucination, perhaps not greatly different from what one might experience post-toad-suck. Or lick. (Some suckers lick.)

A full-fledged anxiety dream lasts longer, though the "length" of a dream is somewhat imponderable, something on the order of asking oneself, "How long is a tapeworm?"

"Too long," is probably as good a guess as any.

So we see that tapeworms could easily be the stuff of Deb's sleepless nights.

But just now we're getting back to Ralph Happler, the young man whose demise was foretold on page 18. Ever since he read "Unyielding," he's been plagued by anxiety. "Am I really going to steal a car and get totaled ~~four~~ three-plus years from now?"

And, "Is there no hope for me?"

Well, who can say? As Oscar Wilde piquantly quipped, "I can resist anything except temptation." It remains to be seen whether this Happler kid has a truly Wilde side and will be unable to resist the allure of a humming red Miata®.

In the meantime he dreams himself into some doozies. The other night it was being chased by a very large predator in the dark. He could hear it but not see it as he raced and raced to get

306 You can't make this stuff up, though someone must have at some point.

307 Page 168.

away, the heavy breathing getting closer and closer, him wanting to scream but unable, wanting to turn to face whatever but too panicked to take a chance, and waking in a pool of sweat, mouth dry, eyes wide, hands gripping the blanket as if there were no tomorrow!

Or, days (actually nights) earlier (but late, if you see what I mean) when he was falling, falling, falling, with the canyon floor rushing up to meet him, only to awaken having landed on the bedroom floor. Did that whole dream happen in the split second it took to descend from mattress to carpet? It had seemed like hours or days of deepest dread. Deepest.

We are, all of us, victims of trauma, with strong evidence that it can be generational. Big or small, childhood or more recent, dispossession of a candy bar or a native land, it shapes who we want to be, perhaps even who we are *able* to be.

Loss of a native land and enslavement? That'll rock you and yours for pretty much ever. I'm pretty sure those of us whose forebears weren't can't begin to imagine the nightmares of those whose were.

It is a heritage one could only hope to somehow erase.

It isn't at all clear that one could hope for more.

It isn't at all clear that it is even possible.

Deracinated

This is the kind of trauma we were mulling on the previous page. Deracinate a plant and you'll almost certainly kill it. Deracinate a person and you kill at least a little of her spirit.

Leaving your homeland is one thing if you choose that path, but quite another if you are deported. This is fresh to mind just now, the Prez having declared the Armenian genocide a "genocide" yesterday on the 104th anniversary[308] of that horror.

I know it's a buzz-kill, but it's worth remembering, I think, that we aren't all "good eggs." Marching about a million women, children and the elderly into the Syrian desert with no food or water? [The current Turkish government claims it was collateral damage in a time of war.] [?] [An accident?] [Really?]

That the Western Asian Ottoman "Young Turks" were evil is clear, but it's perhaps also worth considering that we Western Europeans extirpated an estimated 130 million indigenes from the Americas through deracination, disease, enslavement, starvation and murder.

Would be kind of pleasant to hear an American prez fess up to our own crimes. Maybe someday.

But enough of that wallow. These days we mostly confine ourselves to murdering people on the other side of the planet, which is much more pleasant.

"Nation building!" [See? Much, much better.]

"War on terror!" [A beautful day for a cluster bomb. Ahh!]

Here and now we're going back to the original meaning of deracinated and we're going to revisit Irma Max,[309] the landscape artist we grew to know and love in "A Little Like A Link of Chain."[310]

Recall Irma's trauma regarding the Nile crocodile.[311] When she was in the Peace Corps®? Where she learned to operate a backhoe? Surely, you've not forgotten already!

---

308 April 24, 2021

309 See also page 140 in the current volume.

310 Page 36. *Fifty Wheys to Love Your Liver,* BUB, 2018

311 Ibid. Page 122. See also "Hermes" page 147 in the current volume.

While landscape folks are best known for planting things —think Frederick Law Olmsted[312]—they often deracinate as well: Breaking eggs to make mayo and such like

Last weekend Irma took on one of those Sisyphean tasks that comprise the anxiety dream-demon of a horticulturist's life.

English ivy (EI).

At least being employed to remove the stuff provides a form of job security—there's that to be said. Success is very apt to be temporary, and the tangled vines are more than likely to be here long after we are a pleasant memory or not of whatever eventually finishes us off, be it little green men or a coronavirus, or, I don't know, cane toads? ["Preserve your memories, they're all that's left you."[313]]

A key problem with the stuff is that deracinating EI almost never kills it. [We should be so personally lucky.]

Betty and Reginald Kent bought their current home a couple of years back and knew right off that the ivy had to go. It was all over the yard, way up into the trees, and had even begun its inexorable advance toward taking down the house. Which it will, which it will—assuming fire doesn't get there first. They did make a bit of a removal effort, getting it off the walls, but good intentions are far from enough with a foe like the dreaded *Hedera helix*.

Hence they hired Irma.

Reggie, as is evident from the family name, is of English extraction himself and so experiences a certain hesitancy around claiming *Hedera helix* as one of his own, much prefering the common name, "bindwood." Or the other, "lovestone."

Both of those labels have an additional appeal to Mr. Kent, which I hesitate to discuss.

What I will say here is that Kent's forebears bear some level of culpability regarding the deracination of mine, who were forced out of Scotland in the Highland Clearances. To the degree that generational trauma is a factor I entertain little doubt that my own powerful distaste for injustice could be rooted there.

---

312 Reminding us of Sally in "Sally's Fourth," (*Can We Have Archaic and Idiot? 2,* BUB, 2009/2019) " Sally believed with Frederick Law Olmsted, and Lord knows, I believe they are right, that fireworks prevent tyranny. So, for that matter do—probably—gay militias, free public libraries, political cartoons and religious heresy."

313 "Bookends," by Paul Simon, from the Simon and Garfunkel album *Bookends,* 1968.

My peasant stock escaped to Ireland just in time to enjoy the Great Famine. Ain't we got fun? It's been common practice to blame that mess on a blight, but there's also evidence that absentee landlords were exporting potatoes to England while the Irish (and Scottish emigres) starved.

Turks have no monopoly on evil.

"Why are you hesitant?"

About what?

"Kent's whatever."

Well. As I mentioned in *Waist Not, Want Knot,* "If [bondage] floats your boat you're moored in the wrong marina." [Page 20.]

"Bondage?"

Bindwood? Lovestone? I think you can put two and two together. Betty too. Far be it from me to criticize what goes on in my neighbors' bedroom. Out of sight and (mostly) out of mind.

So the removal of said plant matter presents a somewhat schizoid dilemma in the Kent household. They don't want the trees to die and they certainly don't want the house pulled down, but the way the vines sensuously, lasciviously, wrap their grasping tendrils around naked limbs is, well, let's call it what it is: erotic as the dickens to our passionate/fastenate couple.[314]

Reggie's nickname for Betty is "Wisteria."[315]

Just sayin'.

And in the heat of things she sometimes whispers "kudzu" in his ear.[316]

Drives him totally wild!

---

314 For those of my readers whose boats this floats, chalk up another steamy scene.

315 Another invasive, FYI. He sings it to her in the same tune as "Perfidia," (Spanish for "perfidy", meaning *faithlessness*, *treachery* or *betrayal*) a song written in 1941 by Alberto Domínguez (1911–1975), a Mexican composer and arranger born in the state of Chiapas. This makes us think that Reggie has further twists in his approach to eroticism, does it not?

316 Another invasive. I think we're seeing a pattern here.

Shut Down

Well the last couple were grim and gritty, so let's see if we can't cheer things up a bit. Obviously this whole ... what are we calling it now? This whole can of worms? No. I think that's too trite, as well as *too positive*. I mean, if you're headed to the fishin' hole with your cane pole, there's nothing you'd rather have in your other hand, except maybe a beer, in which case where's the bait? Which reminds me of an ice fishing joke. As such things will.

We already used "steaming heap," which still makes me laugh. Reminds me of Firesign Theater®. As such things will.

Ah. Got it. Obviously this "whole Tupperware®-ful from the back of the fridge with green stuff spreading across the gelatinous surface of something we had for supper a month ago"—this whole *assemblage*—is about giving up. Ceding, if that has slipped your mind.

But shutting down can be a successful cede of a certain unsubtle sort that veers off in a cheerful direction! Say you were aboard the Space Shuttle Challenger®? Shutting down ten minutes earlier would have made for a much happier day. Much.

O Ring! O Canada! O-Reo®! [Isn't that what the wicked witch's guards were chanting as they marched around the castle? In the *Wizard of Oz®?]*

"O-Reo®, oh, oh. O-Reo®, oh, oh." Cookies, cookies.

[And this back when "product placement" wasn't yet a "thing."]

Here, though, making a fresh start, let's find a new friend.

Anyone want to pitch me a letter?

"Q."

You aren't Q-Anon curious by any chance? I mean, the security team was supposed to screen readers.

[Fellow in back shakes head.]

OK.[Whew!] Let's see. Quentin. There's a name for you! And since I was kind of knocking the Brits on page 177, maybe give them another chance here. We'll go with Quentin Bigsbee and see where that gets us.

Bigsbee was born in Londonderry and landed here as a boy, when his mother was promoted from her employer's British to their New York headquarters. He grew up in Glen Cove on Long Island where he was, by turns, teased or envied due to his "funny" accent—and actually both. Those who covet are often dismissive of that which cannot be obtained.

[As in thinking one's neighbor's *alluring* wife is kind of a Plain Jane after being turned down regarding a nooner.]

In high school the theater teacher made great use of Q's accent by casting him as Macbeth (though of course Macbeth was a Scot), and as Alex in her production of *A Clockwork Orange*.

[She was, naturally enough, removed from her post after that one. What was she thinking?]

But that taste of footlights and stage makeup and make-believe left a lasting impression, and Bigsbee was able to do some summer stock at the Gateway Playhouse® in Bellport in his late teens and worked his way into some lead roles in his twenties. He began to dream big! [Ed. Note: If you want him to be taken seriously he should study the Method at some point.]

He landed a spot in a New Haven production of Tom Stoppard's *Travesties* in 2005 (May 11 – June 5) and was well on his way.

[Fellow in the back raises hand.] Yes?

"Bo-ring. What about the ice fishing joke?"

Hey. We're only just getting to the good part.

"We're about to fall asleep back here. Joke? Please?"

Whatever.

So this group of Minnesotans are out on the ice. Some have little huts that they've dragged out with snowmobiles. Others just dress for the weather and sit on little stools, dropping their lines through the holes they've carved. They formerly used axes but these days most of them go with electric chain saws.

Wow, look! The ice must be two feet thick!

There's smoke coming out of the shacks, so you know the well-to-do fishermen have heaters and are quite comfy, while those less well-off brave the zero-degree chill.

"Not funny. Come on, dude."

So, none of them are having any luck. Just freezing their butts, at least the hutless ones, and biding, and biding, and most sipping from hip flasks, which is not really a good way to fight the cold. It may make a person *feel* more accepting of circumstance, but it isn't really recomm ...

"Get to the point, man."

So a boy shows up, chops himself a hole in the ice—with an ax!—drops a line and pulls out a fish in just a few minutes. Then another. And another. And another.

The men begin to cast questioning looks at one another. Finally one stands and goes over to the lad.

"Yer doin' pretty good, son."

"Mmm-hmm."

"What's yer secret?"

"Mmmp um urms um."

"What's that?"

"Mmmp um urms um."

"I don't understand."

Now, more insistantly. "Mm md mmp um urms um!"

"You being funny with me kid?"

Boy spits into his mittened hand. "Keep your worms warm!"

Are you satisfied? I didn't claim it was a *good* joke.

Where were we? Ah, New Haven.

Travesties was the last production of the Long Wharf Theater® 2004-2005 season after which the place shut down for the summer. But that's not the shut down which is the subject of the current natter.

Bigsbee went back to Glen Cove, feeling a little let down. Returning to the folks' house is never a 27 year old's highest goal, though it's always good to have a port in a storm. Oh, there were auditions upcoming: New Haven. Off Broadway. Toothpaste ads. (He's got nice teeth.) Clothes modeling? (Oh, geez, no. I mean, sure, for slinky women who get paid the big bucks. But a regular guy in Fruit-of-the-Looms®? Not so much. Probably gets paid in 6-packs of Jockeys. Or gotches.) Then too, there was the Method class he'd been meaning to take, and he signed up.

As with so many acting wannabes our boy waits tables between gigs, and the acting comes in handy. As does the accent. Patrons of high-end restaurants are suckers for a Brit and a bit of a flourish with the pepper grinder, a little bow with a nod of the head, "At your service *mademoiselle,*" and so forth. "As you wish, good sir." Brother can he lay it on! And tips on large tabs o dadd up!

On the occasion in question a fabulously wealthy matron was treating her best friend to a lavish meal. I'm sure you can just picture it, so I won't waste perfectly good pixels on description.

They were well into their second bottle of *Pinot Grigio,* with its "bouquet of garden herbs, subtle rose petal, complex fruit flavors, and lovely oiliness, followed with mouth-filling complex fruit flavors." [Bisbee's words, not mine. I'd be more inclined to say "tastes pretty good," but then I wouldn't get the big tips.]

The women were practically eating out of his hand at this point, as I'm sure you can well imagine.

After Bigsbee had headed back to the kitchen, Loretta leaned close to Francine and said, in low tones, "Isn't he something?"

"Oh, indeed!"

"I sometimes think of taking him home."

"Doesn't he have a car?"

"Not what I mean and you know it."

"You are so naughty Loretta. You wouldn't though, would you? Really?"

"Wouldn't be the first."[317]

"Loretta! No! You ...?"

"Francine," [insert dramatic pause, then firmly] "Yes."

Eyes wide, her friend emits a little gasp and a giggle. "Loretta, you are *so-o* naughty!"

Then the lights went out, nor were there candles, the local fire marshall having clamped down after that blaze at Angelo's®. You remember? That Italian place down by the bay, candles in *Chianti*[318] bottles with the wax all dripped down on the straw baskets? He blamed the candles and the straw, but we all knew he was on the take.

Think about it. The owner was in hock up to his belt-line and the fire happened in the middle of a blizzard, when it was approximately impossible for a firetruck to get to the scene, when there wasn't a chef or a server or a patron in the joint and, please note: If there were footprints in the snow they were covered in a heartbeat.

What would you guess happened? [Insurance fire, hmm?]

Bigsbee reappeared, flashlight in hand. "*Jeunes dames,*" [I told you he could lay it on: French with a Brit accent? Positively slays 'em.] it is my "teddibly" sad duty to inform you that we have had the deep misfortune to experience a power outage."

[Now I'm sure you think that this will require shutting

317 Here's another lurid and steamy to keep your attention on the story.

318 Making it the second Italian wine mentioned in just two pages!

down the establishment and that this is the "shut down" advertised in the title on page 179. But no.]

"Can it be corrected?"

"I fear not. I've been instructed to inform you that your meal is on the house and that I am to escort you *belles dames* to your waiting carriage or coach, as the case may be." [Laying it on again.]

The women picked up their purses and Bigsbee guided them, unsteady as they were, to the exit, accompanied by other servers with flashlights and diners in tow. There was some grumbling, but most realized that on top of the free eats, they'd been dealt a delicious tale on which they could dine out for weeks. Have you ever been the beneficiary of a free meal, a meal not to mention one carrying a price tag well up into the hundreds, due to a blackout? [I thought not.]

When the trio reached Loretta's Mercedes® Bisbee first opened the passenger door for Francine, then lighted the way to the driver's side. As he reached for the door handle, Loretta pressed two Big Bens into his hand and whispered directly into his ear, "You handsome man. When do you get off work?" [The *Pinot* is clearly talking here. So she probably said it in Italian. "Sei un bell'uomo. Quando esci dal lavoro?"]

Our boy handled the situation with surprising aplomb, and isn't that a British-sounding word? "Aplomb." If we were describing his reaction in a more American-esque idiom we'd more likely say that he "Kept his cool." Right? Or, "He was pretty chill."

Bigsbee made his little bow with the signature tip of his head, turning the flashlight up toward his chin which made him look a little, whaddya call it? Ghoulish? "You flatter me so, *madame*." [We see here the shift from the earlier "young ladies"[319] and "lovely ladies"[320] to a term that seems to imply a bit of seniority in the woman he addresses. "But I fear it is likely to be quite late."

Breathily, "I'm a night-owl."

"Quite, *quite* late. Good evening, *madame,* and good night."

"Well!" Loretta thought but did not say. "Well!" Then aloud, "And good evening to you, Quentin. And good night."

Shut down, or what?

---

319 *Jeunes dames*
320 *Belles dames*

Cutting Loose

This one could be about, oh, I dunno, a "volunteer" Aztec virgin who is tied up in the priests' waiting room pending the winter solstice[321] celebration when she will be relieved of her heartily beating heart? They've drugged her with some sort of herbal concoction that has her kind of sleepy. Having a hot date with an obsidian knife is not entirely a "positive," even if you've been promised a happy-ever-afterlife. The sedation is intended to reduce a certain inclination to escape that had proven to be all too common among the "volunteers."

But what's this? Her boyfriend? What's he doing here? And what's that in his hand? Hard to tell in the dark. It's glinting a bit in the moonlight presently peeking through a crack in the adobe wall. [I mean, I think it's adobe, but it's hard to tell, looking back from six or seven centuries in the future.]

Apparently the Aztecs were pretty keen on this sacrifice stuff and sort of imagined that it was a routine necessity, most particularly in times of pandemic. If they were right [and who are we to judge?] then why did we wait so very many months for a Covid-19 vaccine? Just sayin'.

"Psst. Chalchihuiticue,[322] it's me. Ixtli."[323]

"Huh?" [Clearly doped up.]

"I'm here to rescue you."

"Wah?"

"We can run away together."

"But blessing ..."[324]

"Chalchi,[325] I've got a plan."

"Huh?"

"They only use political prisoners and virgins, right?"

---

321 Or whenever it is that the Aztecs thought to be a good time for a celebratory sacrifice. I'm making this up as I go along.

322 A real Aztec girl's name. I'm not making this up.

323 Ditto, only for a boy.

324 We see here that she's remembering the day's events. Sacrificial "volunteers" blessed babies and so forth as part of their official duties leading up to the monthly heart stopper.

325 Hypocoristic. Much easier to say.

"Wah?"

"What if you weren't a virgin?"

I think we can see where Ixtli is going with this. But credit where due, he *is* trying to save her life.

Oh, and moving in with a telephoto lens, I can see that he's gotten hold of one of those ceremonial obsidian knives![326] Next he'd probably cut the ropes and carry her away. "Go on, take the honey and run!" [Just think what Steve Miller could do with a story like *that!*]

But that isn't what this fable is about. Recall that the third word upslope was "could."

No indeed. Today's paper[327] has spun me back and back to the other side of the world. Ancient Egypt![328]

Ancient Egypt!

Egyptologists have discovered a pregnant mummy! My gosh! I mean, I know the dead are sometimes said to be sleeping —viz:

> "*One of a broken pride, in the search for heart's desire,*
> *One after life in far-away London and Paris*
> *Was brought to her little space by Ella and Kate and Mag —*
> *All, all are sleeping, sleeping, sleeping on the hill."*

[I don't know, maybe call it a "failure of imagination?" Edgar Lee Masters killed off a bunch of people in "The Hill" but didn't include any sacrificial virgins. Y'know?]

So, anyway, mummies are sleeping but who knew that they were "sleeping-around?"

[Oh, geez! That is so judgmental of me.]

Anyway, this mummy resides in Poland whence it was whisked in 1826, and was long referred to as a "mummy lady." But in the early 1900s, based on translation of the hieroglyphic inscription on the ceremonial packing box, it was believed to be that of a male priest, *Hor-Djehuty.*

Apparently some tomb raider switched crates, because an x-ray taken in 2015—but only carefully analyzed four or five years later—has revealed an anomaly in the pelvic area to be a 26-30 week fetus. [Insert pathos.] The mom-to-be was apparently in her 20s. [More of the above↑.] [Male priests are only very, very rarely pregnant.]

326 Twice already in slightly over one page of make-believe!

327 *New York Times®,* 3 May, 2021.

328 I'm sort of an equal-opportunity anthropological enthusiast.

The strangest thing in the article, to my way of thinking, came from Dr. Alexander Nagel, a residential research associate in the anthropology department at the Smithsonian National Museum of Natural History®. Nagel told the *Times*® that papyrus from around 1825 B.C.E. revealed that materials such as honey and crocodile dung were used as contraceptives.

You've got to wonder, don't you? I mean, I don't go looking for this stuff, and here we are dealing with crocodiles again. Guess those Ugandans (see page 144) better keep the croc pit clean or Hermes won't be churning out any handbag fodder!

But the *Times*® article is edifying in other ways as well. Dr. Nagel said about 30 percent of infants died within their first year of life during ancient times in the Nile Valley. After learning of the discovery of the pregnant mummy, he said he was intrigued about what further study could reveal about Egyptian beliefs concerning the afterlife of unborn children.

Gosh, that's tragic. The thing about babies is that they aren't always a good idea in the first place. Of course, if you're losing a third of them right off, well then, obviously, you need to make more. But, as a friend was telling me, literally, just a little more than twelve hours ago, regarding her research on mid-19th-century French foster care policies [you see right there the high quality of the friends I keep, and just one more reason I dedicated this book to her], here's a "thing." At around the time the pregnant mummy waltzed into Poland, France was in terrible financial shape. Many people were destitute. Lacking resources to care for children, women were killing their newborns.

That sounds horrific, but imagine the conditions that would make a woman think that quick death was kinder than keeping the child alive. So the government, filled with good intentions toward the babies and with population depletion a significant problem, passed laws. Women were required to give birth in hospitals and to stay there for eight days afterward, breast feeding. The goal was to forge a bond between mother and babe. Then, if the woman still decided she just could not provide for the kid, she had to produce the hospital-verified birth certificate when turning the youngster over to the state-run foster agency.

A downside was that the foster agency had to be paid dues which many could not afford, plus many *did bond* and decide to keep their progeny ... only to have them starve to death later.

Which reminds one, as it must, of Chairman Mao's *Great Leap Forward*® in 1959. It was verifiably reported that as ~~the~~

~~forced~~ *the celebrated* social change created famine, all the while propagandizing the bounty that ~~the forced~~ *the much desired* collectivization had produced, people were trading children so as not to eat their own.

But that's not what this story is about either, so sorry for the buzz-kill. Like I say, I just report. I mean, I make most of this stuff up, but the stuff I don't make up keeps beaming in. Fiction is what it is, but it isn't like toothpaste with an "invisible protective shield," or whatever they used to call it, "around your teeth."

So, now, back on track.

We were focused on "cutting loose" not long ago, and so we will proceed. For you regulars I want to assure you regulars that we're **not heading back** (emphasis mine) into the vast catalog of rope and tangles and string tricks thoroughly dissevered in *Waist Not, Want Knot*. Nay nay.

[An aside: In your "normal" conversations do you ever use the word "dissever" without thinking of Poe? Nor do I. His "can never dissever" was choice.]

[Oh, and for the record, Chalchihuiticue and Ixtli "went down south and they're still running today."[329]]

But, "the story."

When we last checked in with Bgisbee he was politely declining a tryst. We note here that the offer was made by a not unattractive somewhat older woman, and that Bisbee was professionally obsequious, given that he was both an actor, long in the habit of obeying direction, and a server, long in the habit of "serving." Surely he could have "played the part" of a "lover."

Could he not have?

Yes, he could have.

Did he feel some sense of remorse, declining her offer?

And, if so, what drove that remorse?

This, I'm pretty sure, will raise up Bigsbee in your esteem machine. [And don't think it isn't important to an author to have his fictional characters, or at least some of them, thought well of.]

Bigsbee didn't feel bad about turning down the offer of a, [Hmm, what's the modern idiom? Roll in the hay? No. Kind of old-fashioned. Hookup? OK.] hookup for fiduciary reasons. For one thing, he's not for sale—outside of, clearly, working for tips or for hire as an actor. For another, at the moment that he declined Loretta's "come-on" he didn't know he had two Big Bens in his

329 Or, rather, were *then.* Clearly they now "belong to the ages" as what's his name said about Abe Lincoln.

fist. It was dark. He only knew he probably had currency of some sort. A tip.

It's an interesting moral consideration, is it not?

I mean, most of us, most of the time, like to imagine that we're "not for sale." We do have our pride.

What if Bigsbee had known that Loretta had just "tipped" him $200? Would that have changed his response?

No, it would not. He did feel a tinge of sadness, however, for the lonely lady Loretta. Tsk. Tsk.

Oh gosh, we've already "enjoyed" an old joke in this story. Can we handle another?

[Hand up in the back.]

"It better be a better one."

Well, at least this one is "relevant" to the current tale. So here goes.

A man approaches a woman in a bar. He introduces himself and asks, "Would you sleep with me for a million dollars?"

"Are you serious?"

"Yes. I have it here in my briefcase. In cash." He holds up a heavy, clearly stuffed item of luggage.

She pauses ...

Nah. It's worse, so forget it.

But, I repeat, the answer regarding Bigsbee is "no." No negotiation whatsoever.

Bisbee is one of my good eggs. Yes, he'll take direction. Yes, he'll be obsequious in dealing with restaurant patrons. But, no, he'd not engage in carnal relations with a person of either sex with whom he did not have a deep emotional bond. Had he known she'd just tipped him $200 his answer would have been no different. Had it been ten times that and he'd known? Ditto.

If Loretta had, instead, suggested something less sexually suggestive, he might have taken her up on it.

"How about coming over to my place for a late-night game of chess?"

He would have agreed to that in an unknived heartbeat.

Or, maybe, "There's a light bulb out in my ceiling fixture that I can't reach. Any chance you have time after work?"

You see? To that he would have assented. He's kind of Boy Scouty regarding helpful, courteous, kind, etc. and so forth.

"And kind of bo-ring."

OK. You in the back: Take a chill pill. We're getting to the good part now.

"It better be, or I'm outta here."

Bigsbee has a *pet hamster*. Named Goliath.

Didn't see that coming, did you? Wowza!

The thing, or at least one thing, about having a personable companion animal the size of a medium baking potato is that he, and Goliath is a "he," is pretty portable. So, yes, Goliath was in New Haven when Bigsbee was moteling it during the *Travesties*® run mentioned on page 180. Goliath heads into the Big Apple with Bisbee when he has business there. Actually, and don't tell anyone about this, because it would seem kind of, I don't know, superstitious? Bigsbee often had Goliath in his pocket when he auditioned. He had the notion that having a hamster in your pocket was good luck.

[Before you instantly "pooh pooh" that, my take is that you should try it yourself. We really don't have data regarding how may lottery winners had a hamster inside their shirts when their lucky number was drawn. Nor, for that matter, how many "volunteer" sacrificial virgins were passed over while they were thoughtfully stroking their hamsters. Or gerbils.]

[Also, please note: I am not in the pocket of the hamster industry. No one could pay me enough to tout hamster husbandry in my serious artworks. To which I might add, there were no financial incentives provided regarding my discussion of guinea pig recipes in "Knot My Problem" and "Surgeon's Knot."[330]]

[Oh, and also, Goliath is at this point long past his expiry date. All regular pets dash through our lives way too fast. Those that regularly outlive us ought not to be adopted in the first place. Pets require responsibility.]

Where was I? Likely asleep. Yesterday was a long one. I don't think I need to make excuses.

This hamster business reminds me ... but that can wait. No doubt you want to move along with Bigsbee and so forth.

You in the back, with your hand up? I know what you're going to ask, so, this:

Goliath was *not* Bigsbee's idea. Not long before the New Haven gig he'd been seeing a woman—not to clutter things up with new names to remember, let's say it was Brenda Ellington, the squirrel monkey lady, before the monkey, and before she

330 Pages 20 and 137. *Waist Not, Want Knot,* BUB 2020. So I guess I have headed back into that morass. Sometimes I can't help it.

moved to Cullowhee—I mean we didn't give her either a backstory or a speaking part last time around, and who knew that she'd arrived in Cullowhee after a stint in Long Island? Surprise, surprise!

So Brenda and Bigsbee were mildly itemized for a while. Brenda was teaching at the community college where Bigsbee later took a class in the Method. They mildly clicked and kissed and diddled and so forth. [Score another steamy scene!]

Brenda's companion creatures at the time were a pair of hamsters, and as rodents are wont, they made more! If there's anything cuter than a Pomeranian puppy or, say, a red-spotted newt eft, it has to be a *wee wittle* hamster!

Before she cut loose and took the new job at Western Carolina U., Brenda gave Bigsbee the pick of the litter.

"Sweetheart," she said [finally gaining a speaking part], "I want you to have a hamster to remember me by."

Aw. That is so damn touching! Has anyone ever given you a hamster?

Nor I. Or is it "me?" "Nor have I ever been given?" or "Nor has anyone given me?" Personal pronouns are a challenge, hamsters or no.

The rest I think you can figure out for yourself.

Crumbling

I'm sure some among you are quite convinced the cookie already has, and I can live with that. But you're still with me at this point so I don't believe you've completely lost hope that something, oh, I don't know, maybe something "entertaining" will emerge? Something to have made your investment worthwhile?

We only have about ten pages to go at present, so at least its clear that if anything "valuable" is going to pop up it won't be too very long.

The thought of crumbling often takes me back to a sea wall in Old Mexico. If memory serves, and I believe I've demonstrated that mine is approximately fathomable, it was between Mazatlán and Puerto Vallarta, but I could be wrong four decades on. It was definitely a sea wall I was standing on, and a crumbling one at that. A sign at the site suggested that the sea wall was not old, that the project had been completed only a few years back. Yet, as I already mentioned, it was crumbling.

The crumbling part is not why the memory remains so very clear. The crumbling was entirely incidental to the bubbly nubbin of the extant memory, and therefore is not the "crumbling" to which the title of this story refers. But that title certainly took me back. As titles will. As titles will.

You see, I was standing on the sea wall, as I believe I've already mentioned, when a heavy-set fellow tourist came over to chat. When I say "heavy-set" I am being kind. He was shirtless and his enormous belly was jutting out over his Bermuda shorts like a ... searching for a simile here ... oh, snap! got it! ... like a really huge gut hanging over a belt line.

It turned out he was a retired cop.

[My instant impression was that he ought to have steered clear of at least *some* of the donuts.]

But, you need some backstory before we proceed.

I was 30 at the time and had worn my hair sort of shoulder length for a decade or so, though that would give you the impression that it hung to my shoulders, which it did not. *Very* curly. Sort of a white-guy Afro would be a more accurate description.

Right up to three days before the crumbling sea wall.

Preparatory to heading south, my partner and I with her brother and sister-in-law drank some margaritas at their home in Tucson. Several. Ample. Sufficient.

Also 30, Susan's brother was what some people refer to as "prematurely" balding, though the rationale for that term escapes me. Is there a "maturely" balding? And wouldn't that refer to someone who is balding but accepts it in a grown-up way? Which would mean that "prematurely" balding refers to balding on a person who doesn't accept it in a grown-up way?

You see?

Anyway, his response was to shave his head. That is, so as to make the bald thing intentional, which, to my way of thinking, is a very grown-up way to approach the situation. Meaning, via the razor-sharp logic exhibited in the above, that his "premature" balding was actually entirely "mature."

So in the cheerful and, frankly, jocular spirit of the margarita-induced mood, he "dared" me to shave my head.

I shrugged and said, "Why not?"

Then the three of them sheared me and shaved me.

[By the way. If you've never shaved your head you really ought to try it some time. It offers a huge sensory shift. The sun. The shower. The breeze. Oooooo!]

[Also, if you shave your head, I would suggest not heading to the subtropical beaches of Mexico in immediately ensuing days. Between the sunburn and the no-see-ums, daily shaving became kind of torturous. Plus I was dry-shaving due to uncertainty about some of the water sources. But that's a different story altogether.]

So. I was standing on a crumbling seawall looking like what we had come to refer to as a "skinhead," and a retired cop stepped up to chat. Being friendly-disposed when he told me about his former employ I asked him what he most liked about the job.

"It was those damned hippie demonstrators," he said. "When I hit them on the head with my nightstick it sounded a lot like smashing a watermelon."

O ... K.

It was immediately apparent to me that absent the head-shave the man would never have spoken to me. I had put on a new costume.

I shaved my head for the next eight or ten years. Nothing like a costume to bring out the "best" in people was my theory.

Then, too, there's this.

Now, I don't want to be accused of cultural insensitivity here, nor of painting others with too broad a brush. Nor of falsely demeaning an accepted societal "practice." Or whatever.

But, following that illuminating conversation on the crumbling seawall, I spotted some construction sites further south, where young children, maybe 8 or 10 years old, were pouring concrete while men, presumably in charge, sat on lawn chairs in the shade. I think I kind of thought "a little more supervision might have been useful regarding the seawall."

This week a rail bridge in Mexico ... but on with the story!

You'll recall, surely, Franklin Franklin, the scalawag chestnut vendor we met on page 13. Do you not? Of course you do. His betrayal of all things noble and upright launched us on this deep dive into the offering up, the granting of grants, the abandonment of what wanted leaving, the just plain letting of goes that wanted letting of, and so forth. When you come down to it, Frankie has been the only *really bad egg* in this entire, what were we calling it?

Oh, right. This "whole Tupperware®-full from the back of the fridge with green stuff spreading across the gelatinous surface of something we had for supper a month ago."

"Cappy Thornsen!" [From the guy in the back.]

You're right. I left him out. I think it's pretty clear we don't want to hear anything more about Franklin *or* Thornsen, those bad apples in the story barrel. So we've weeded a bit (to further mix up the metaphors.)

Then we have the jurors. Well, well. We've probably had our fill of that crowd, too. I mean, they were so *wrong*. So. So. At least we can feel some sense of justice served when their verdict was upended, can we not?

We can.

And then we had various bit players, none more a "player" than Quentin Bigsbee, and none less a "bit" than what's her name. Loretta's dining companion. The one who giggled.

There was Ned Fowler as well, but he's had his turn in the sun. Penny and Tim Morgan were even given speaking parts! As too have been most of the others. But looking back I see that we left Larry Monroe in a bit of a lurch.

He'd arrived at Jan Bender's place bearing a bottle of nice wine and a lovely bouquet only to find her gone. He thought he had a dinner date but found he was the sole attendee at a wake, phoned 911, and went outside to wait for the arrival of the authorities, all the while humming that BeeGees® song from page 172.

> "Here I lie, in a lost and lonely part of town.
> Held in time, in a world of tears I slowly drown.
> Goin' home, I just can't make it all alone.
> I really should be holding you, holding you. Loving you, loving you."

This would have only been their third or fourth get-together, so it would be a hard stretch to paint him as really heartbroken, but it was obviously a shock. Also, it's easy to overdramatize at moments like that, and for gosh sakes, Larry, *you weren't lying down.* He was standing around kind of mentally drumming his fingers.

As recent as their new interest in each other had been, he didn't even know if there was someone else he should call. He thought he remembered something about relatives in Asheville, but that was sketchy. It might have been an ex she mentioned. She *had* been married at some point.

He certainly had no license to rummage around in her desk for whatever clues might have been found, and to whatever degree he was tempted in that direction, he knew the timing would be unfortunate, what with the police and who knows what all headed in his direction. For that matter, when he thought about it, he realized he was feeling a little *protective,* like he was doing Jan *a favor,* guarding her *stuff* so that some "authority" figure didn't rifle her effects.

Authority figures are not always good eggs.

Like most of us Larry was feeling a strong urge to tell somebody, anybody really, what had happened. He tried a couple of friends but neither picked up. He was pacing the driveway when he noticed an across-the-street neighbor sweeping her sidewalk. He crossed the road and introduced himself.

"Hi Larry, I'm Lisa Mickelson."

"Do you know Jan?"

"Sure, we've been neighbors for several years."

"I had a date with her for dinner tonight."

"We chatted this morning. She told me someone was coming over. She baked a pie for you but Brenda's monkey got into it."

"Brenda's monkey?" That sort of nonplussed him. Then, "I hate to be the bearer of bad news," [not, we know, actually true—he really, really wanted to tell *someone*]. "Jan is dead."

"What?"

"I knocked and she didn't answer so I went in and I found her on the kitchen floor."

"Are you sure?"

"Oh, I'm sure."

"Did you call someone?"

"911. A half hour ago. They're sure taking their time."

"Did you tell them she was dead?"

"Yes."

"Well, that explains *that*."

Larry suddenly realized he was still holding the flowers and the wine bottle. "These were for Jan." He held out the bouquet. "You can have them."

"Why, thanks. Thank you. Would you like to sit on the porch while we wait for the ambulance or whatever? I'm kind of in shock."

He nodded and held up the wine. "Do you have a cork screw?"

Which, of course, she did or the story would have dead-ended pretty quickly.

Soon Lisa was telling Larry what she knew about Jan, that she did, in fact, have an ex in Asheville, named Merv Condon, who was probably the best contact. There were adult children too. Then, as such conversations will, things veered. [There's a limit to how long a person wants to talk about a corpse in a neighbor's kitchen.]

Three hours sped by and Larry finally announced that he thought it might be a good idea to call 911 again, just to check.

Surprise, surprise! [I know you've been hoping something "interesting" would happen.] *Surprise!*

The 911 system connects phones to addresses and rather than write down Jan's address which Larry had duly provided, the automation had pulled up Larry's! The authority figures had gone to his house and finally broken in when there was no answer, thinking that, who knew? It could be one of those murder/suicides where the perp kills, calls and then takes himself out. They went in with guns drawn and came “this close” to shooting Larry's Bassett when the old fellow shuffled out to meet them.

Ten minutes after the second call the authorities pulled into Jan's drive and Larry went over to talk with them and make a “statement for the record” and guard Jan's stuff. Soon they'd collected the corpse and he returned to Lisa's porch.

“It's really late and I'm hungry, can I take you to dinner?”

“Why, yes, that would be lovely. I've kind of blanked on cooking, I could have made you something.”

Lisa proved to be much more in Larry's “lane” than the dear departed Jan which somewhat diminished any sense of loss for either of them. This is OK. As the Firesign Theater® sketch had it, “Shoes for industry! Shoes for the dead!” [As a practical matter, Lisa bought a couple of pairs of Jan's shoes at the estate sale!]

Here's where we interject the obligatory “do's.”

Lisa paints when she's not working. Little still lifes.

Larry whittles when he's off work. Little people. Also still.[331]

See how aligned they are?

After a suitable ramp up they will certainly become what we have come to refer to as “itemized.” Diddles and all.[332]

Now that we have Larry in a happy place, and Lisa too for that matter, though she just showed up on page 194, so it isn't like we'd left her in a “lurch” way back on page 172 the way we did him, we can move along with the story part of the story. But we'd better hurry!

As previously mentioned, the “correct” size for a book is 200 pages, making this the last page of fabulous adventure and derring-do. [We have to leave room for Book Club Questions and the obligatory Author Interview, as well as one set aside for Shameless Commerce and then a blank, so you know it's over.]

So here's what you really need to know about Larry. This Larry, I mean, not the bike repairman. He's a scuba enthusiast! Every year he goes down to Costa Rica for two weeks to dive in the turquoise waters amidst schools of brightly colored fish and sea turtles and rays and sharks and jellyfish! This coming January he's going to take Lisa with him, assuming the plague is under control. [I found some blank space on page 105 so head back.]

331 If they were, say, puppets? Not still. Not so aligned, see?.

332 Wanted to get one last steamy scene in here before we check out.

Book Club Study Questions

Standard Questions:
Huh?
What?
You mean?

For deeper consideration:
Plain or peanut?
Trepanning anyone?
Carcharodontosaurus! Run away! Run away!
Nice *Noblet®* or *Nice Noblet®?* Split the difference.
In what did Cook & Co. part ways with *Cristobal Colon?*
Tapeworms? Compare and contrast.
Diddle? [Heating up the book club, we are!]
Have you developed empathy for Aztec virgins?
For which worms should one *not* call animal control?
Are Egyptian cotton sheets worth the extra?
Wasn't this collection just wonderful?
Do you suck toads?
Would you like to? Or is licking more your *œuvre?*
John Lennon or Bare Naked Ladies?
Thacyline?
Would you buy a used obsidian knife from this man?
Toward what is sunset's bloody sword pointed?
What should you feed your breeder salamanders?
Can you use "dissever" in a poem?
What do we mean when we say "itemized"?
Do you think that Happler kid is going to steal the Miata®?
Can you name the largest kangaroo that ever hopped?
Do mummies sleep around?
Daddies? (Sorry. Couldn't help myself.)
What kind of pictures do you think the guy who taught math sold?

No, seriously, wasn't this book just the ticket to a National Book Award®? What with all the *française* and *français* and so forth? With the particle physics? And a Klein bottle? When was the last time you read a short story that included a Klein bottle? Or a pregnant mummy for that matter? Or tapeworms?

This, my friend, is the real deal! [*vraie affaire!*]

Author Interview

Did you *really?*
Not saying.

Why?
Pleading the Fifth.

Because?
I have a right to remain silent.

Did you ever stop to think?
Once.

And that didn't change your mind?
Well, kinda. I at least saw through the paradox. Kind of a Zen moment, really. It both is and isn't at the same time.

Do you do anything worthwhile with your time? This is shaky.
I mull.

Is seeing believing?
No. "Believing begets seeing." See what I mean? Note observation by what's his name on page 73. Or was it 97?

Do you have anything else to say in your own defense?
Temporary insanity. Runs in the family.

Good intentions don't count. Don't you know that by now?
But they feel pretty nice.

Shameless Commerce Page

Self-Evident: We Hold These Tooths

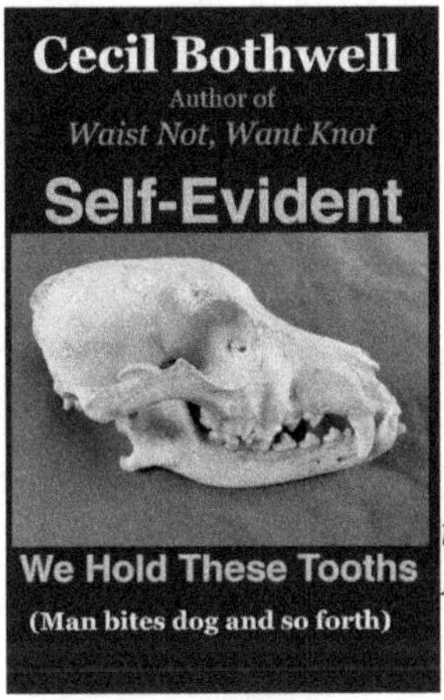

If you loved this book, you need to read the prequel.[336] The stories here left you with a lot of questions. Unanswered questions.
But now you know where to go.
So go already.

336. And the pre-prequels, *Waist Not, Want Knot, Seize You on the Dark Side of the Moo,* and *Fifty Wheys to Love Your Liver.*

Whale Falls: An exploration of belief and its consequences

What do you believe and why? How do your beliefs affect your view of, and relationship with, the world? A very personal examination of the author's journey through a lifetime of adventure and abuse and resolution.

This page intentionally left blank in order
to inform the reader that the book has ended.
The mostly vacant pages that follow are an artifact
of the manufacturing process.
-cb

CPSIA information can be obtained
at www.ICGtesting.com
Printed in the USA
LVHW020016280423
745413LV00009B/274

9 781088 113004